GET YOURSELF
TOGETHER
FIRST

GET YOURSELF TOGETHER FIRST

Events From The Diary of A Child of A Crack Addict

GAVÁTA

XULON ELITE

Xulon Press Elite
2301 Lucien Way #415
Maitland, FL 32751
407.339.4217
www.xulonpress.com

Printed in the United States of America.

ISBN-13: 9781545649060

If you are a recovering addict or an addict desiring the path of recovery, and perhaps you're trying to play make up, or forcibly restore relationships with your children or family, - Or maybe you are the child of an addict who feels like there has been too much hurt and pain, to forgive...

THIS BOOK IS FOR YOU !!!!!!

DEDICATION

First giving back to the source of my thoughts, dreams, and the very epitome of my being, I dedicate this composition to God. Being of principal importance in this earthly realm, the subject matter of the first book I have ever written, I primarily dedicated this writing to my mother, Mrs. Regina B. McCollough-Hargrove. Next, to my loving deceased grandparents, Bishop Walter "Sweet Daddy" McCollough, and First Lady Saint Madam Clara B. McCollough; to my stepfather who has been my daddy, Jiamé J. Hargrove; my four amazing children, Isaiah, Christian, Carlos Jr., and RéJene ; my beautiful grandchildren, Naomi, Zaye'mari, Micah, Kamari, Armani, Chloe, and Serenity; to my best friends, Aaron Easterling, Sirena Whittington, and W. Tavon Johnson, you all are both loyal and God-sent, and I appreciate your encouragement and prayers. I genuinely and authentically love all of you. Rev. Cheryl Mercer, you have been more than a mentor, confidant, advisor, visionarian and a friend. Thank you for putting up with me. Where would I be without you?; To an Amazing Woman of God, Rev. Lettie Moses Carr, God used you to deliver me, cultivate and let me know that I am able to be that which He called me to be.;

Ms. Karen Fulton, you are my cheerleader, supporter, mentor, encourager and intercessor, thanks for your love through it all. To the one who mothered me when my mom was unable to, the late Mary "Aunt Sissy" Hill; the one who fathered me teaching me the values of life and who the true and living God really is, my late uncle, Rev. Charles Leon McCollough; and of great appreciation to my covering, my parents in the Gospel, Archbishop Alfred A. and Co-Pastor Susie Owens (Greater Mount Calvary Holiness Church). You all have consistently, authentically and genuinely loved me, supported me, prayed for me and encouraged me. I am nothing without CALVARY !!!

DISCLAIMER

This is a true story. However, some names, titles and places in this book have been changed to protect the identity of those involved.

FOREWORD

Normally the "Foreword" of a book illustrates a strong view of the writing, eloquently written from one powerful individual. Instead of giving platform to the perspectives of others, I want to leave as much room as possible for you to gain what you can from these written expressions. Therefore, I decided to gather statements and quotes from a variety of personalities, which reinforce an array of points I hoped to convey.

> *Forgiveness is the art of admitting that I am like other people*
>
> *— Mother Teresa*

> *Love is not a good part of your life; it's the most important part... Love is the secret of a lasting heritage.*
>
> *— Rick Warren*
> *Author of Purpose Driven Life*
> *Saddleback Church*

Discontent is the first step in the progress of a man or a nation

— *Oscar Wilde*

One of the hardest things in your life is having words in your heart that you can't utter

— *James Earl Jones*

It's a choice- not a chance- that determines your destiny

— *Jean Nidetch*

This heart operation cannot be accomplished in sterile religious clinics or on the comfortable theological couches of the modern church

— *Mark Hanby*
Author of You Have Not Many Fathers

As I reflect on the painful portraits that hang down the hallway of my life my memory is flooded with experiences that have shaped my life... In one sense, even my dad and I eventually reconciled and we now have a good relationship, I do wish I could erase that part of my life. But I also see it has made me the person I am today – emotionally stronger and better, able to empathize with others in pain

— *Erik Rees*
Author of S.H.A.P.E. Saddleback Church

I've learned that people will forget what you said, people will forget what you did, but people will never forget how you made them feel

— *Maya Angelou*

A moment of self-compassion can change your entire day. A string of such moments can change the course of your life

— *Christopher K. Germer*

Faith is taking the first step even when you don't see the whole staircase

— *Rev. Dr. Martin Luther King Jr.*

Don't receive condemnation when you have setbacks or bad days. Just get back up dust yourself off and start again.

— *Joyce Meyer*
Author of Battlefield of the Mind

Alone we can do so little, together we can do so much

— *Helen Keller*

Love costs all we are and all we will ever be. Yet it is only love which sets us free.

— *Maya Angelou*

A broken heart never mended handicaps us terribly when we're challenged to trust.

— *Beth Moore*
Author of Breaking Free

The dark does not destroy the light; it defines it. It's our fear of the dark that casts our joy into the shadow.

-Brene Brown Ph.D., L.M.S.W
Author of The Gifts of Imperfection

Before making assumptions based on prior knowledge, compare what you've learned to what you observe around you. – Often our drives and tenacity come from the places that stink in our lives.

— *Bishop T.D. Jakes*
Author of INSTINCT
Pastor of The Potter's House

TABLE OF CONTENTS

INTRODUCTION

MESSAGE FROM THE AUTHOR

As you turn the pages of this book, I can only ask that you keep an open mind. The stories you will read are not pretty and will not be dressed up with eloquent words. The only way for you to fully appreciate the restored relationship between my mother and I, is for me to explain the details and to try to get you to understand our despondency. These events of hurt, grief, and brokenness will very likely make you angry with my mother, *an addict of 24 years*, and leave you feeling sorry for me.

PLEASE DON'T !!!!

I am sharing with you some of the most intricate incidents of my past. I elected to leave *no stone unturned* because I need you to thoroughly understand some of the pain, voids, and disappointments of my life, so that you can fully appreciate the healing. I wanted to try to convey to you in words, the sin-sick mind of an addict, and how it affects all those connected.

My mother left me in excellent living conditions. A Christian home, with more love, morals, ethics, discipline and *things*, than most children can get, even from a two-parent household. Nevertheless, it did not matter. The maternal longing was still present. I still wanted my mother.

This testimonial does not have a chronological format. Hence, these compilations of stories are categorized by specific feelings, expressions, actions, situations, incidents, or those involved.

I hope that my readers will gain a different perspective of the process of restoration and forgiveness after *recovery* and during the "one day at a time" sobriety walk. It is my goal for addicts to realize that once you are serious about your sobriety, your love ones will forgive you without a formal apology. They will love again. Respect again. And, trust again. You don't have to spend the rest of your life trying to play make-up for the time you did not have it together. For the unforgiving loved, it is my desire for you to understand that we all have pain, but the blessing is that we survived it and are alive to tell the story and to forgive. We're able to help and encourage others by affirming the change, which we have observed in our "recovering-addicts-life".

I urge you to identify "in" and find apart of you and your story in this book. Take note that you too have had an addiction that someone had to forgive. It may have been a relationship, a job, sex, men, women, television, the internet, food, shopping, stealing, gambling, drinking, partying, excessive spending, attention seeking, etc. While I never used drugs, nor smoked cigarettes, I am now able to see my indiscretions through continued self-evaluation. In doing this, I am able to recognize what could potentially be considered an addiction, immediately bring that thought into captivity, and eliminate self-deception. No one is exempt from this because no one is perfect.

It is my prayer that this writing enriches the need and provokes urgency for the rekindling of relationships, as well as the ability to grasp that compassion is a primary component for convalescence of the heart.

Today, my mother is an awesome woman of God who has been clean since December 11, 1999. She is a missionary, play writer, former Sunday School teacher, and facilitator of the youth department of the United House of Prayer for All People, in Washington, D.C. She has performed in various capacities surrounding counseling, case management, and social work. Being a drug addiction counselor, and a sponsor of many, keeps her involved and giving-back, to the place of desolation she was delivered from. Having four children, twenty-seven grandchildren, numerous great-grandchildren, she is able to be effective and comfortably fill these shoes without being indebted or motivated by guilt. Most importantly to me, she is the one who raised and ushered my youngest daughter into being my first child to ever attend college. Prior to my grandmother's death, the late Madam Clara B. McCollough, trusted her wholeheartedly with some of her most valuable and sentimental possessions, as well as relying on her for several matters pertaining to her health.

There has been times when, I have found myself in compromising or impoverished predicaments, and my mother was the one that was there for me, no matter how near or far we are in distance.

3

Regina B. McCollough-Hargrove is my mother. Our struggles, turmoil, and trials are the hard, blackened, seemingly invaluable rocks that ushered her into being *my* priceless diamond that I wear in my heart and on my smiling face when I am not wearing any visible jewelry.

FORGIVE AND RESTORE, OR DEVELOP WHAT HAS ALWAYS BEEN A NEED

Gaváta

SECTION I:

WHY?

CHAPTER 1

"I wanna go too! Get off of me. They have so much fun at Mamma's house!", Gaváta (Vá) expressed in her most broken, screaming, child-like voice.

"Sit down, Gal", her grandmother demanded. Aunt Sissy, the loving middle-aged woman who nurtured her in love and mere presence, simply guided her near, cuddled her, and then looked in Gaváta's eyes only to say, "We love you honey. I work hard, your granny works hard, and we want you to be somebody. Your mother's life is over. She destroyed it." With a smirk, she softened her tone, and went on to say, "But you can get your education and go on to be in the ice capades or in the Ms. America Pageant".

Gaváta, the youngest of four, was taken and raised in her grandmother's home from the time she was a baby due to Regina, who was her mother, having a drug addiction. Her two oldest siblings lived with her mother and her other older brother was being reared by another family member, whose residence was within walking distance of Regina's home.

"But Sissy, I don't want to. I wanna go to Mamma's house and play in the rain like my brothers and sister. I want to have fun and go to concerts to see New Edition and Prince too. They get to go to the corner store when they want to. Other kids are outside for them to play with on the playground. You don't understand!" the child tried to reason with her aunt.

"Now you listen Gaváta, we love you. You have food to eat, toys, a clean place to sleep, clothes on your back, and more dresses and shoes than the average child could imagine [for church], and you want to go down there in that mess. Your mamma's using that ole stuff. Rob, Ruth, and Tony don't know where their next meal is coming from. Their clothes are dirty. They wish that they were in your shoes. They wish they had what you have.— Sissy, put her down and stop pacifying that mess. — Vá, go get ready for your bath so you can go to bed." And, with those echoing, stern words from her grandmother, Gaváta lowered her head and went off into her room, while looking back only to see Sissy still standing in Granny's room, shutting the door so they could continue their grown-folk conversation.

CHAPTER 2

"OK Vá. Yes! Yes! Yes, you can go with your Momma this one time.
Don't make it no habit." Aunt Sissy apprehensively granted her request.
"Oh! Thank you! Thank you! Thank you! I'm gonna miss you so much",
Gaváta jumped around happily and squealed with much excitement.
She was going to be able to spend a weekend with her mother and
sister. She just knew that she was going to have so much fun.

After the car turned from 6th Street on to "N" Street, Northwest,
it didn't even have the chance to come to a stop before Gaváta jumped
out, darting through to playground of the McCollough Canaanland
Apartments, owned by their church, The First United Apostolic
Church for All People. Taking her night bag inside, was of no concern because she was finally outside with other children having fun.
Night fell and eventually they had to come inside. Ruth, her friend
Alonda from church who also lived in the church's neighboring apartments, and Gaváta, all went in, ate sandwiches, and prepared for bed.
Now, this was the part she dreaded. "Why do all the lights have to be
turned out? Why they gotta listen to all of this slow music, so loud,
to go to sleep? Why cant they just cut the television on? Dang, it isn't

no TV in Ru-Ru's room." In missing Sissy, these thoughts penetrated Vá's mind. As hard as it was, she finally got off to sleep, only to be awakened in the middle of the night to Alonda's light skinned breast being guided into her mouth saying "Suck it Gaváta, suck it." Tight lipped, she shook her head in refusal and tried to scratch her big sister, Ruth, with her toenails, to awaken her, but she never did budge. At first light, Gaváta snuck on the phone and begged Sissy to come and get her after telling her what happened. The phone eventually rang back, and Ruth answered. It was Sissy telling her what had occurred. Ruth was so infuriated and openly displayed it by beating Alonda profusely and then dragging her home to her mother by her hair. Ruth needed Ms. Dessoda to hear what her teenage daughter had done to her baby sister. After Gaváta repeated it, they left, but it wasn't over because Sissy was on the way. Sissy arrived and fussed and ranted and raved and went back to Alonda's mother to re-confront the situation.

In the end, Sissy had two questions for both Ruth and Gaváta. "Where in the world is your mother and when's the last time y'all saw her?" Upon learning that after she picked Vá up and dropped her off, she had not been seen since, Sissy became infuriated. She grabbed *her only concern* [Gaváta] and all of her belongings and stormed away. She blustered verbal degradations of Regina for the entire fifteen-minute ride home. Gaváta quietly wondered if she would ever be allowed to go with them again.

SECTION II:

BROKEN

CHAPTER 3

In a peach satin dress, she fell asleep on the queen size bed of the Days Inn on New York Ave, Northeast, in Washington, DC. Her white tights were still on, but her black patent leather shoes had been removed. The mattress was so firm that entering or exiting the bed caused no disturbance to anyone else lying there.

In the wee hours of the night she was spooned by a man who was unrelated to her. She felt her dress rising. The rough hands and force of a man trying to get to her prize through these little girl tights. Maneuvering through material, garments, and underclothes, in search of her folds of pure flesh, his hands found what he searched for. Round and round and round, he massaged her purity. She blinked a little and looked over only to see her brother Rob, at the far end of the bed in a deep sleep, clueless to the invasion of his baby sister, that was taking place. He was so near, yet at that moment, so far. Only three years her elder, and not even 140 pounds, yelling was out of the question. Through blinks and peeks, and peeks and blinks, she began to wonder, "Where's mamma? Why are we still here? OK, OK, OK, let me think ..." Was this thought process a way to remove herself mentally, from what was happening?

"OK, focus Gaváta", she told herself. "Last night we went to The Gospel Hummers of the Sky concert. When we left, Ma told me to ride back with Mr. Mitchell, my godfather [so she said] and the band while she went to get us all food. She came back to the hotel and fed me and Rob, right here in the room with Mr. Mitchell. He cut the television on and told us that he had to go to one of the other band member's room to discuss business, and for us to keep the door locked, because both he and Mamma had keys to get in. He also said that Mamma would be back soon." All of these reflections ran through Gaváta's mind as she still wondered why and how she was in this position *now*. "Go back to sleep, go back to sleep, go back to sleep, go baaa...." she continued to repeat until she drifted off to sleep, yet again. "Vá, get up, — Imma get in this case. I pick locks good." she woke up the next morning to hear Rob quite excited, while he fumbled the combination to the briefcase that sat on the dresser. Wiping her eyes, she looked around processing the events of the last 24 hours. "What's wrong?", Rob asked.

"Nothing. I gotta pee-pee.", she replied.

"Well then, go on." he nonchalantly shrugged.

Sitting on the toilet, urinating, having to wipe and clean where this Grammy Award Winning Gospel Recording Artist fingers had fiddled about, just hours before, seemed surreal and embarrassing of the sorts. As she washed her hands, she stood dazed by the water pouring from the faucet, until her concentration was broken by the yelp of joy from Rob. "Oh my God! Look at all this money. Dang, it's jewelry in here too." She came running out, "Oooo! Let me see. I want a ring. Is there one with a "G" on it? Why do he got so many rings that are just alike, with different initials on them? You think he got godchildren wherever he go? Wow, that's a lot of money." Rob looked over at his little sister who was full of excitement with mounds of questions and said, "Yep! And I'm about to get paid. I would give you some stuff but you tell Grandma and Sissy everything." "Na Uh! I promise. I want some stuff too cuz I never get nice stuff for school, only for church", she plead with her brother. "Look Vá, I'm only taking a little bit because he's not just a singer and guitarist, but he's the treasurer for the whole band so a lot of this money is the band's, not his", he explained. With a look of disturbance but a natural female intuition to persuade, she said, "I know why you should take it all." He looked at her as if to say 'go on', but letting her voice her argument. "Mr. Mitchell got in the bed with me last night and touched me all *down there* but you wouldn't wake up." With a look of dismay and gritted teeth, and the need to ask, Rob was able to get out one word, "What?" — And there sat Gaváta telling her brother, it all. Within seconds, 'patience' left the room and he vented, "I don't believe this bull *crap*. Mamma always leaving us somewhere. Every time these celebrities come to town, there she is being their all-night-drug-connect. Oh! But hell naw! This nigga gon' pay."

Two hours later Gaváta and Rob were taking the streets of Georgetown in D.C. by storm. Everything from TROOP branded leather bomber jackets, to full GAP sweat suits, with Gucci linked gold chains, they had it. Rob later parted and went to his hang out in the downtown-Shaw-area of Northwest, where he could show off his 'come-up', and Gaváta headed home to Allison Street for a much desired bath. Feeling refreshed and *apart-of*, she got dressed in some of her new clothes and decided to go to the corner store, just to be seen, by all of the "Hustlers of the 3rd and Upshur Hill". Never having clothes this expensive for leisure and street wear gave Gaváta an added confidence. She practiced her walk on her 2 ¾ block stroll. When she turned the corner from 3rd Street on to Upshur, her walk emulated a cross between the swags of Run D.M.C. and L.L. Cool J. The black Gap sweat suit was baggy and tomboyish, *if you will*. With hands in her pockets, she felt all eyes focused on her, if nothing but for those 60 seconds. Three stores and a Chinese fast-food-take-out-joint, became points of destination, one-by-one. Satisfied with this brief status of popularity, and for once not being viewed as the daughter of the crack head Regina, Gaváta returned home to hide her most prize possessions before Sissy or Granny could arrive home from work.

Later that evening, she heard, "Ding! Dong! Ding! Dong!" The front door bell wrang as the pitter pats of the rain beat profusely on the black concrete streets. "Hold on, I'm comin'." Aunt Sissy yelled, as she proceeded to the front door. "Hey Genie", which is what Aunt Sissy called Gaváta's mother, instead of Regina. "Hey, Lil' Mamma" she replied, using her own special surname for Sissy. Through a mouth twisted to the right and lips poppin', Regina asked, "Where is that dang bless-ed Gaváta and Rob? They stole all Mitchell Harding's money and jewelry and most of that stuff belong to the band. The manager of The Gospel Hummers of the Sky is talking about going to the police before they leave town. They'd better give me what they got left, so I can take it back to him, before they windup in jail by tomorrow. He sent me in cab. It's waiting outside." In utter shock and disgust, Sissy's only response was, "What? Let me go up these steps. Vá!, Ga-Vá-Ta!, Váta!, Moo-Moo! I know you hear me." Faking sleep, she ignores her aunt's call until she is eventually shaken awake. "Maaam. What? Huh? I don't know." Bombarded with questions, this is how she answered. Saddened by the discovery of her misbehavior, Gaváta cried as she unveiled the items she began to love within the last 24 hours. She could never lie to Sissy or disappoint her any further. After Sissy gathered everything from Gaváta , she met up with Regina in the vestibule, to see what all she had gathered from Rob who was staying in the basement. Off she went with the clothes, jewelry and receipts. No money was left. A heart sickened girl looked from the upper level bathroom window as the things that gave her temporary healing and validation, were loaded into a black and orange car labeled, Capitol Cab Company. "It's so gloomy and rainy outside. Momma's probably about to go and sell that stuff. Who is that on the other side of the cab door? Tony? My brother Tony? Awww... look at him. Mamma got him on crack too and he's stealing our stuff from the opposite side door, taking everything out that she is loading in. She's so high that she don't even see him. Dang, Tony can run. Look at him go, off into the graveyard that sat behind St. Paul's Episcopal Church, over the hill, there goes all of our stuff.", Gaváta thought, — she felt, — she observed, — and she ached.

Sissy came to bed and looked at Gaváta and asked, "Vá, why would you do that. I'm so embarrassed."

"I'm so sorry, but you just don't know what he did to me." She used this to justify her behavior, but then she decided to share. She told Sissy everything. With eyes of pain and vengefulness, she listened intensely Vá told every detail. All she could say to this broken child was, "Oh, Honey! I'm so sorry! But you can't tell no one else.

Nobody! OK?" Gaváta reluctantly agreed knowing she'd repeat this story again and again, until she was heard.

Monday morning soon came, the walk to Rabaut Junior High was slow and purposeful, but quite to her, in spite of all of the noise of the other children around. Sometime before the lunch bell even could even ring, Gaváta Smith was sitting in front of her 7th grade guidance counselor telling this story. The D.C. Metropolitan Police came and took her somewhere she couldn't identify and made her repeat the story again. That person took her somewhere else and she had to tell the story again. Over and over, all day long, she relived the horrors of that night, remembering that her mother left her in the hotel with a man, only to be violated. And then, came back and took the very possessions that gave her some comfort. Late that afternoon, possibly right before night fall, her grandmother, Madam Clara B. McCollough, First Lady of The First United Apostolic Church for All People, was called to come and get her. She knew that the consequences would be dyer. Of course, due to her grandmother being the Commander and Chief of the home, sent her all-time Sargent at Arms, Mary A. Hill a.k.a Aunt Sissy. Sissy was the "Olivia Pope" of the house. She would handle this by being the voice of reason, to make this go away. On the ride home, Aunt Sissy wasted no time in warning Gaváta that her grandmother was beyond upset. Granny's concern was primarily about '*embarrassing the McCollough name*' and not having the church or her grandfather's name dragged through the mud. Secondarily and surprisingly, she worried about ruining Mr. Mitchell's career. Gaváta listened but zoned in and out, feeling unsafe, unprotected, inadequate, and insufficient. She was even more so, confused about how to equate these events and feelings with being as loved, blessed and fortunate as her grandmother insisted that she was. But somehow, the crack addicted Regina, was able to convince this Christian Woman of wisdom and discernment that all of the truth in which Gaváta told to everyone, were mere lies to cover up her thievery.

CHAPTER 4

———————•———————

"What's happening right now? I'm confused! Where am I? Oral Sex!" Her eyes began to blink open, only to see the ceiling and light fixture to her very own bedroom." "Wait! What the...?", she thought as she began to clear her mind and answer her own questions. Looking down at the face between her thighs, she almost lost her breath, but the tears began to stream back into her hair as she laid back down in disbelief and shock.

"You gotta be kidding me.", riddled through her head like an astronomical mathematical equation, "Rob? My own brother! The one who comforted me through me being violated the *first* time. Naw! It just can't be! – Yell! Say something! Say stop! Stop thinking and speak!"

Softly she finally whispered, "Rob, Rob, Stop. I think I hear Sissy coming. – I gotta pee." He got up and then said, "Hurry up back." Knowing how to jump, skip, and circumvent every creak in those old wooden steps, Vá make her was down stairs to the main level couch where Sissy always sleeps when Granny is out of town. Sissy was in the kitchen and when she returned to the couch, there Gaváta sat with a lowered head. "What's wrong?", Sissy asked. Of course, she wasted no time in telling her aunt what had just occurred. Without any concern for time, shelter, or safety, Aunt Sissy marched upstairs and said, "Nigga get your stuff and get the hell out now. I don't care what you tell , I'll tell Aunt Clara *(Sissy's name for Granny)* that I put you out myself.", were the next set of words that echoed through the home. Some brief arguing between the two occurred and soon the sound of Rob, with his belongings in tow, came down the steps with him cutting an eye at his victim of the night but never saying a word.

The next day three calls came in. One from her sister, Ruth. One from her mother, Regina. And, one from her Grandma Madam, who was away out of town for the church's Annual Holy Convocation. All of them accused her of lying, once again. None of who believed her. She always knew that Ruth would defend Rob since they have the same father, which has made them extra close. Momma was so high, she didn't even care to investigate. Maybe her nonchalant attitude is reasoned by just what she said, "All of my cousins and uncles did stuff to me too Vá, but nobody talks about it. We all grew up and got over it." Gaváta wondered if this was her mother's was of saying, "Shut up and deal with it." But she just couldn't grasp how and why this illness of drug addiction wouldn't allow her mom to care and feel, as she believed that mothers should. One thing she knew without question, as it had begun to take root into her life and memory, was that granny's position is and always will be, in any matter, that we as a family do nothing to "Embarrass The McCollough Name". Not ever.

So regardless of what happened, *by McCollough Family Law*, it never happened. But then something else happened. Rob Smith Sr., the father of Ruth and Rob Smith Jr., had a child by the woman who had ceremonially vowed to be Gaváta's godmother, Kara. Kara was once the lover of Regina, but gave birth to a daughter by Regina's second husband Rob. Her name is Tasha. A young stepsister for everyone, especially for Rob Jr. And so the cycle repeated, — at not even 5 years of age, her voice resounded and told the story yet again, of who this "Brother Rob", really was.

No one ever apologized even though Gaváta's allegations were validated. Most importantly, she wanted her mother's love, and trust, and for her to believe, defend and stand up for her. But she didn't. All she wanted was her mother, even if she was in a drug-intoxicated-state, she longed for the validation of Regina.

CHAPTER 5

"O.K. Vá, now I'm gonna act like I'm leaving out of the house, but I'm gonna sneak upstairs and hide until you come up there. Go tell Aunt Molly you need Momma's room key to get some of your school supplies out of there so you can do your homework. Aunt Molly is almost ninety years old so she is not crawling up these two long flights of steps. I need to get some things out of my momma's room too, but you know how they act with me. I'll wait until you go in to get your notebook paper and then I'll come in too. But don't worry, Imma give you a couple of dollars for when the ice cream truck comes. Her mother's words were so convincing and flowed so naturally, that Gaváta could only believe that finally she was able to help her mom do *something*. As she approached their elderly housekeeper, Aunt Molly, who had assisted in the upbringing of both she and her mother, she convinced her to give her the keys to Granny's room. She ran up the stairs and unlocked the door, and took a few sheets of notebook paper from underneath the dresser. When she stood up, she watched her mother take money from under the nightstand cloths, television ledges, and in folded up nightgowns in granny's drawers. She remained motionless while witnessing what was taking place. Inwardly she somehow felt that because she was obedient, a bond would develop and her mother would come and get her more often.

As time went on, this became a repetitive course of action. Habitually, another request would be made of her, with a different set of instructions, and each time, over and over and over, she'd follow through while learning the 'art of deception, manipulation and theft'. As often as Granny stayed on the road traveling with and for the church, Regina continued to use her daughter for financial help in support of her addiction. But then the expectation suddenly escalated.

Granny was home! She was in the din preparing for dinner and after a hard day's work, she had sat at the table with her back towards the formal dining room. In her brown Gucci Clutch Handbag, that was placed in a chair at the table, in an adjacent unused dining area, sat three bulging envelopes of money. Each of which were labeled and read of some sort of *Love Gift Offering* from some random occasion, for 'First Lady St. Madam McCollough'. Gaváta's job was to take one, and put it in the designated spot for her mother to grab it. The addict would be watched, not Vá. So, as Regina talked intensely to her mother, the attention deprived child, set out to execute her assignment. When the mission was accomplished, Gaváta sat to take her seat at the dinner table. Regina then said her farewells and began her departure. Her mother escorted her to the front door, locking it behind her. Dinner went well and then Granny grabbed her belongings and headed upstairs to her room. After settling in, she noticed the missing envelope and became absolutely enraged. Being a woman of the cloth, she did not use profanity. But that day, only a fool couldn't fill in the blanks had she chose to be indignant. It was scary and at that time she couldn't figure out how her daughter had pulled this off, because there wasn't any doubt in her mind who had her money. Vá sat quietly and went to her room hoping that her mom would call her or come back soon.

Quite some time later, on a random weekday, she did come and get her and told her that they were going to Portal Drive to see her grandfather. Gaváta was beyond excited because this was a rarity. They arrived there safely and as Regina talked to her father for what seemed like hours, the child sat on the huge California King bed watching and admiring the father in her life. He was dressing in one of his *fine* suits. His dressing area sat off of the actual bedroom with department-store-mirrors-sliding-closet-doors, which seemed to be at every angle, and had floor to ceiling lengths. Grandpa dimpled his tie after putting the gold tie-bar in place. He put on his cufflinks, ran the chain of his pocket clock through his button hole and upper pocket, slid on his rings, clamped on and secured his Rolex, then headed downstairs to his office. Sitting on his nightstand, strategically placed, was a huge bulging #10 white envelope full of money. Gaváta glanced at it once, but had a reverence for who Bishop Walter "Sweet Daddy" McCollough was. Not only was he a father and provider to her, but also, he was the Leader and Overseer of God's Kingdom in the First United Apostolic Church. In her eyes, to mess with her grandfather, was asking for punishment from God, and that she knew that she better not even think about. When they left the house on the long walk from Portal Drive to Silver Spring Metro Subway Station, she endured the "Why didn't you do this or that?" When no answer was given, she was called so many demeaning names. All she could do was lower her head, cry and listen to the mother she loved so dearly, whom she'd do almost anything for, hurt her with harsh, mortifying words. Somehow, because she failed to betray her grandfather, her mother's inability to accept her good behavior, was quite confusing. In spite of Regina's chastisement, Gaváta knew that this time, she had done the right thing.

CHAPTER 6

---·---

"Look Shawdy I like you and er'y thing but you gotta keep dis' a secret for real." Reggie explained to Vá. "I can't lose my job behind us, so you can't tell none of your friends." Reggie was the 25+ year old janitor who worked at Shaw Junior High School on Rhode Island Avenue in Northwest D.C. Gaváta was a 9th grader there at the time, and often skipped school in the morning to travel to the bowels of Southeast and become entangled in a small one bedroom apartment with her over aged boyfriend in Marbury Plaza High-rise Apartment Building. Reggie didn't have to be to work until 1 o'clock in the afternoon, so when she arrived, no time was ever wasted. Every moment was utilized. The things this grown man did to her tender youthful body should have only been shared between husband and wife. But she was being loved by a man and she was being 'desired' above all the rest, *so she thought.*

"Shelly, are you there? Stephanie, girl why you keep clicking over? Y'all are the worse friends to chill wit' on three-way. Y'all are always clicking over or doing something, and then gotta hand up.", Gaváta expressed to her best friends as they chatted on the phone. Then Shelly said, "Oh! I know you ain't talkin'. Me and Stephanie be on the phone three to four hours every night, but your aunt is always making you get off the phone to do this or that and then we gotta call you back."

This was pretty much the lies and deceit amongst the three best friends as they had their individual reasons for getting off of the phone at different times. Eventually the same sort of pattern, became noticeable because the hours in which they would arrive at school, and their excuses for being late, were much too close in similarity. Being quite the clever one, and inwardly feeling that something was certainly off course, Gaváta became mindful and began to make mental notes of both the phone and school inconsistencies. She would pry to see if her friends could tell her minor details about where they claimed that they were, but she always came up empty. Not quite remembering exactly how or when she was able to disengage Shelly and Stephanie's defenses, in due time she was able to catch them up individually, and her suspicions proved to be true. Reggie was sleeping and creeping with all three of them, simultaneously providing the same confidentiality clause. For once, Gaváta chose not to tell-it-all in her moment of hurt and anger. Vengeance arose and she had the perfect plan.

(202)289-4648 was the phone number she dialed when her mother answered, but before Regina could even say Hello, she said, "Ma, wanna make some money?" Of course, the reply was "Yeah! How?" She went on to tell her mother the whole story truthfully. She put special emphasis on Reggie's age and job because that would be the leverage. A couple of days later, Gaváta stayed home and Regina called the school's main office and asked to be transferred to the janitor's office. She then asked to speak to Reggie, citing his entire government name for clarity. When he answered, she confirmed that it was he, by asking matter-of-factly, "Is this Reginald?" When he said, "Yes", she went on to tell him whose mother she was, that she was aware of his age, where he worked, and what type of relationship he had been partaking in with her baby girl. She lied in accordance with their plans and told him that Gaváta was pregnant. In addition to threatening prosecution on the charges of statutory rape, she told him that the abortion was scheduled for the following week and that he'd better take responsibility and at least pay for half of the procedure. That Friday, Reggie caught Gaváta in the stairwell and with minimal words, gave her a white envelope bearing $300. Faking illness, she made her way to the nurses office to use the phone and to the caller on the other end, she simply said, "I got the money. Come and get me." Within an hour, the twisted mouth, dressed up Regina showed up to the office to sign her daughter out of school for the rest of the day. As soon as they exited the school, before even reaching the sidewalk, they split the money and parted ways. Her mother looked back to remind her, "Don't tell Sissy I got you out of school early." Vá waved her off knowing that her mother's only real concern was her next 'hit'. Gaváta then flagged down a cab and instructed the driver to take her to Wisconsin and "M" Streets, Northwest, which was the heart of Georgetown. The next day at Shaw Junior High, when the school bell rang, her 110-pound frame strolled through the baby blue carpeted mezzanine with huge Triangle Bamboo Gold Earrings bearing the name 'Dimples" in them. Her size-two stonewash light blue jeans with a pattern of six frills around each leg, showed off her imaginary excuse for hips, legs and a butt. A navy blue T-Shirt with navy blue

Reebok Classic Shoes, satisfied the fashion of "matching gear", to her outfit. Shelly and Stephanie and Reggie all were opened mouthed when they saw her. She walked by them all as if neither of them ever existed. Little did they know, for the next day, she'd wear the bright red version of what she had just worn in navy blue.

CHAPTER 7

"Boooom-Ka!-Bam!" was the sound the large wooden basement back door made when it was kicked inward forcefully by her high school sweetheart. When it came down, his young, buff, five-foot ten-inch, one hundred and seventy pound physique followed almost instantly, standing on top of the flattened door. With music booming loudly, he began to visually inventory all those who sat in the basement apartment living room, but Carlos scan halted when he locked eyes with this girlfriend. "Gaváta, come here." he motioned as he walked towards the rear bedroom and she followed with her head hung down.

He shut the door as she sat down, and as he was standing atop of her, her repeatedly asked, "What's up?" She hunched her shoulders and remained silent.

He asked again, this time with flailing arms, "I mean, Vá, what's up? You got this nigga Berky in here and you chillin' with him, Rob and Peaches like yall all are one big happy family. How much more do you think I can take? You laid down wit' the dude, I forgave you. I slide over here off the late-night, come through the alley, can see in the basement bathroom and this nigga takin' a leak. What am I to think? I know how your mom expect you to be wit' these dude from around-the-way that's slinging hard but I ain't from L.W. *(Lincoln Westmoreland Apartments on 7th Street, N.W.)*, and I ain't from Lincoln Road, N.E. I can't and I ain't getting down like that no more cuz I'm on this house-arrest-curfew-junk with the courts, try'na stay outta jail. You tell me that you want me here as much as possible because Rob just got out of jail and you're scared cause here living upstairs in the house. But you're sitting down here having couples-night-out with him and his girl and you and Berky. How am I suppose to feel? I'm breaking curfew for you right now. My mother and uncle would kill me if they know that I was out of the house. Come on! Say something!"

She just sat there, taking it all in with tears streaming down her face, one by one. Almost as if a ton of bricks had fallen on her, a screeching wail came forth and then she bellowed, "I'm a whore. Just leave me alone. You have no idea of who I am." The scream was so excruciating that he grabbed her expediently, but not harshly and muffled her cries as he rocked her in his arms. Those in the next room heard nothing. Later, he put her to bed and went to clear out any company. She was renting the basement from her grandfather's estate. This was her personal space and she was allowed to be alone and to say who could and who could not be in her area of the house. Carlos told her that he was stepping out to go to the corner store and asked if she wanted or needed anything. She said, "No". When he returned he had a notebook and ink pen. In it, her asked her to write down every man or boy that she had ever slept with. The longer the list got, the more she cried and felt worthless. For some, she didn't even know their last name. Some had the same first names, for example, 3 named

Eric; 2 named John; 3 named Darryl; two named Carlos, etc. Many were one or two night flings and most were over age 21, compared to her 16-year-old youthfulness. When did it occur? She couldn't believe that between the ages of 11 and 16, she had been so exposed. Surely, he'd walk out now. But he didn't. Instead, they talked way pass sunrise. He listened intently to all of the horror stories about who she'd been with, where and why. Most had some type of connection to her mother or she was trying to get something from them to appease her mom. He stayed in spite of the court order, and this to her teenage eyes, was the second boyfriend who had ever really loved and cared about knowing who she really was. But, who would he become in her life, and was it worth this one night tell-all?

SECTION III:

OH NO! HERE SHE COMES!

CHAPTER 8

"Work the walls, Work the walls! 6-40 workin' da walls, yeah, 7th -n-Taylor", was the lyrics of the song that the live Go-Go band sang at Celebrity Hall a.k.a. The Black Hole Night Club on Georgia Avenue. Whenever the block was mentioned and a specific intersection was called out, all the chicks that represented that area, swung their hair weaves and danced even harder. Pickle, Cecil, Mike, Eric, Manny, and Man-Man were just a few of the guys who not only sold drugs on 7th and Taylor, but they also went to the Go-Go to dance, party hard and represent their area. Gaváta a.k.a. Dimples, her cousin Kimi, and Kimi's best friend Mariam, were the female groupies who always accompanied them. Gaváta had to work extra hard, to look the par and to fit in because all week, these were the same group of dealers her mother brought drugs from. She'd be laughing and playing with everyone and look up, and there she'd see her mom, walking expeditiously, bouncing along on her personal mission, toward the group. A cheerleader frilled jean skirt purchased in Miami, Florida by her grandmother was one of Vá's most prized possessions. There weren't too many items in her wardrobe that people actually complemented her on, but this skirt was above the knee, almost mini, short and cute. She squinted her eyes to get a better view, hoping that she did not see, exactly what she saw. In a 1980's style satin purple church blouse with red and green flower designs in the chest area, her mother moved closer and closer in distance. Hanging from her waist, was the new skirt, Gaváta loved so much and upon her feet were leaning white Reebok Classics with purple shoelaces. Matted to her head with gel was her short wavy hair and on her forehead a line was made to the side as if it was an oversized patch of baby hair taking the place of bangs. On her face was the $.99 blood red Wet & Wild lipstick that had been used for her lips and blush. Not knowing what to feel, what to say or where to go, Gaváta stood still and endured the laughter, and everyone talking about her mother. What was even more hurtful was the joking fact that Vá and her mother wore the same clothes. She greeted her daughter as if they were unrelated, motioned a dealer away from the crowd, got what she came for, and off she went.

It really didn't matter where Gaváta went, what school she attended, how many new friends or crowds she tried to hang with, similar incident always occurred. From 7th and Taylor to 3rd and Upshur. From 3rd and Upshur to 9th and Crittenden. From 9th and Crittenden to 2nd and Decatur. From 2nd and Decatur to 5th and Kennedy. From 5th and Kennedy to 14th and Upshur. From 14th and Upshur to 11th and Park Road. And so on, and so on. Vá ran and she hid, but with every new area she wet to came a new man, -- a new man with sexual expectation, while they provided the minimal things she wanted and supplied the drugs her mother required. "When does it stop, Will it ever stop?" this is what Gaváta often thought.

CHAPTER 9

⸻ ⸻

"Gavàta get upstairs and go to bed." was the awkward command of her mother standing in the foyer of the main level in the home to which she was raised at 300 Allison Street, Northwest. "No, you can't tell me what to do! I'm going to get back on the bus and stay at Uncle William's house for the night with Aunt Sissy.", Gavàta rebelliously responded. Regina tried hard to get her teenage daughter to obey but was met with much opposition.

Grandma Madam had a stroke and had to move in with her husband, Granddaddy McCollough on Portal Drive since that home had maids, cooks, chauffeurs, caregivers and a service elevator to enable granny to move around. Sissy still lived at the family's Allison Street home but when there were transportation issues or the snow would be too heavy to travel off of the steep hill where the house sat, Sissy would often take Và and they'd spend the night at their distant-family-member's home. Uncle William's house was less than half of a block away from Sissy's job, the dry cleaners that she owned, and it was also walking distance to Shaw Junior High School.

This day, Gavàta had taken the bus back to Allison Street Northwest to get some more clothes and more of her belongings. Due to her procrastination by being on the phone with neighbors and friends, night had fallen and her mother happened to come to the house and decide to be a boot-legged disciplinarian/enforcer.

Gaváta was holding to her position that she was going to leave back out, so Regina tried to swat and spank her child. Vá looked her mother in the eye asserting that she had no right to beat on her, and that she had never been there to raise her or to be a mother to her. This did not deter Regina from trying to make this child obey. At the first "wack", Gaváta picked up the phone and made two calls. The first one to 9-1-1, to scream child abuse and to tell them that her mother was on crack abusing her. The second one was to Aunt Sissy to tell her all that had taken place. When the police arrived, they spoke to Sissy, who was still on the line, to tell her what had happened. A debate arose regarding who actually had legal rights to the child. Gaváta ran upstairs and came back with a paper that she kept up under her mattress. It was a document from the D.C. Superior Court where she had gotten in trouble for hooking school due to being teased about her mother's addiction. The truancy officers had reported her absence and she had been released from court into the custody of a responsible adult vowing to keep her in school and ensure her regular attendance. 'Mary A. Hill' was the signature on this legal court document. She signed on the line as the person holding the position of "legal guardian". "Hurt, shock, dismay, disappointment" are a few of the words to describe the look on Regina's face. Not even Aunt Sissy realized the weight and validity of this document, but it would hold true and be the parental paperwork to keep them inseparable for years to come. No one could tear them apart. The police allowed Gaváta to leave knowing that she was returning to her legal guardian. "Relief" was the sentiment of her exhale as she boarded the #62 METRO Bus, taking her back to where Sissy's loving arms awaited her after this dramatic ordeal.

CHAPTER 10

———————•———————

"Iiiiiiiiiiiii, Yes in deed, yes in deed!" Well this is the quote that preceded much laughter as Michael Boone bopped along the carpeted mezzanine of Shaw Junior High. There was always an entourage trailing behind him, of both male and females. This was the only male Gaváta had ever seen people flock behind other than her grandfather and Michael Jackson, so there was obviously something that Michael Boone had that everyone felt that they needed to be near him. She could never figure it out and didn't waste time on trying to.

It was the third week of her 8th grade school year. Other than her cousin Kimi and a few kids from her church, she didn't know many people in Shaw at the time. She knew that Boone was out of her league, so she never gave it a thought.

A few weeks thereafter, approaching the soda machine, her cousin was pulled away. "Yo, Kimi, who dat? What's up with her?" Mike asked. Kimi instantly went into hook-up mode. At first sight, Gaváta thought that he had a peculiar look. She later realized that resembled a young Forrest Whitaker.

Mike was the perfect gentleman. Her being three years younger didn't matter. He dated her, respected her, protected her, walked her to the front door, listened to her and took time with her like no other man had ever done in her life. He gave her money like she had never seen before. He bought her nice things and loved her without reservation. Their teenage relationship flourished rapidly.

And it never fails. Here we go again. Yes, he sold drugs. Yes, he made a lot of money. But, was this a reason for Regina to call the corner phone booth for him more than Gaváta was calling for him? Was this a reason for her to start coming to the latter part of town to 14th and R Streets, Northwest? Could Gaváta ever escape this cycle? When she'd call, she'd learn that he just hung up with her mother. When she arrived, she learned that her mother had just left. When Mike picked her up sometimes, she'd discover that the car was a rent-a-rock from one of her mother's get-high-buddies. 'Relief' was what she desired and eventually her saddened look, told her boyfriend just that.

"Look baby, we gonna get a hotel room for a couple of nights and chill out, OK? Can you get away? Can you talk to Sissy? Is she going to let you go? Talk to her, ask her, I like Sissy and I don't want her worried about you. OK?" was the words Boone spoke to her gently while uplifting her head with his pointer finger. She promised him that she'd take care of it and be ready. When Friday night arrived, she assumed that they were just getting a ride as he opened the door, put her in the back seat and got behind her. Up front was her mom and her friend. They arrived at the Best Western Envoy on the upper end of New York Avenue, which is the hotel strip of D.C. When she saw her mother get out of the car to check them in, and Mike gave her the money, "Oh No, to the tenth power", was what reverberated through her mind. But, she took it all in stride, knowing that within minutes, it would just be the two of them alone. She watched intently as Mike paid her both money and drugs in exchange for the key to the room. Inwardly, she wondered if he had been charged for her too. Quickly removing the last thought from her mind, she flopped on the bed, enjoying her evening. After much laughing, playing, eating, watching T.V. and sex, they both fell asleep in one another's arms, listening to Bobby Brown's song "Tender Roni" which had been set to repeat on the boom box they had brought along. In the wee hours of the night, she heard a knock at the door and he got up to answer. She heard her mother's voice, and knew that she was coming back for more drugs, so she faked like she was still asleep. At daybreak, while she got in the bathtub, she heard the door again, and again he answered fulfilling her request. Gaváta stayed in the bathroom until her heard her mother's voice no more.

The relationship continued but at one point, he became distant. Hurt by the fact that she knew that he was cheating, she accredited his infidelity to him being tired of trying to take care both of her as his girlfriend and her mother's drug addiction.

Undeniably, he was her first love. He fathered her first child, Isaiah, and admittedly she will always love him.

Even today they're the best of friends and have a vow of love until their dying day.

CHAPTER 11

"Come on Gaváta, were gonna be late. I don't know what's taking you so long. You knew that we had to be on time this Sunday. Your Uncle is going to kill you if you're late today." Her Aunt Sissy said these words as she hurried along to get ready for church. This was a special Sunday. D.C. Delegate Eleanor Holmes Norton was coming to the church, to honor her for being a teenage mother, pregnant with her third child, graduating and maintaining a 3.8 Grade Point Average, through it all. She marveled this day. In spite of her difficulties and how much she endured being verbally persecuted for embarrassing her grandfather's name, she'd have a platform and be laurelled for the good she did, in the midst of her mistakes. In her excitement, she got herself together in one of her best Sunday outfits, and on the drive to 215 51st Street, Southeast, she mentally rehearsed what she was going to say, when given the opportunity. Sissy talked and encouraged her all the way to the service. They were both thrilled. Upon arrival Gaváta was escorted to the front pew by the ushers and Aunt Sissy humbly sat on the end of the second pew. After the preaching, and after the offering, and after the singing, and after the announcements, and all the other general business of the church, the Honorary Ceremony was the next event to take place. About halfway through Delegate Norton's speech, Gaváta looked up towards the alter/pulpit. Lo' and behold, to her amazement, coming through the exit door behind where the ecclesiastic body sat, was none other than her mother. Regina's mouth was twisted, she was bouncing, her face was flaking from dry skin, and the word 'high' couldn't even equate the dimension in which it seemed that she was on.

"....And, I just want to give special accolades and honor to Bishop McCollough's granddaughter who maintained Honor Roll status in spite of being a teenage mother. She somehow saw past her obstacles and pressed forward to be successful and to achieve what life has for her. Today I call forth, little Ms. Gaváta Smith." This is a summation of the introduction given by Delegate Norton. Gaváta got the microphone and began to verbalize her appreciation for Aunt Sissy, Uncle Buddy, Grandma Madam, and Aunt Maude (Uncle Buddy's Wife). She then went back to talking about how much Sissy did for her to help her with the children, sitting up night after night to help her with her homework and also she spoke about how much Sissy did to support her financially though all of these difficult times. Without looking back into her mother's face, Gaváta could feel her mom's eyes burning the back of her head. So with almost the faintest of a whisper, she simply said, "... and I'd like to thank my mother, Regina, for her love and support." As Gaváta went to take her seat and the crowd began to clap and whoop, close friends and family got in line to hug and congratulate her. Yet, through the noise, she could hear her mother repeatedly saying, "That's my daughter. That's my baby."

"How dare she act like she has anything to do with my accomplishment. How dare she try to take any credit. How dare she act like she has helped me or my babies in any way." These were only a few of the many thoughts that bombarded Gaváta's mind on that hot summer day. In the midst of being paid homage to, there was a cloud that hovered around and weighed heavily on her heart, but by being taught to be a lady at all times, she smiled and masked the pain that was rumbling in her young heart.

CHAPTER 12

———⊶⊷———

Isaiah (Zaiah)

November 22, 1991 was a rainy night. The show '90210' was playing on the television. It was coming to an exciting 'you-gotta-wait'-til'-next-Thursday' ending, when Gaváta jumped up in both joy and amazement, when all of a sudden, warm water began to run down her thigh and it would not stop.

"Sissy!" she yelled, "I'm peeing and it won't stop." By Sissy not having any children of her own, she wasn't sure what was happening, but she quickly called Grandma Madam.

"A'nt Clara, this chile' here is peeing on herself and it won't stop." she reported to Granny.

"Two Dummies!" Granny yelled, "Mary, get that girl to the hospital, she's bout to have that baby on you."

After a few more phone calls they were on their way. Star, Isaiah's grandmother for 14 years, who in 2008 after a real life "Maury Episode" was found out not to be, is the one who picked Gaváta up and drove her to Washington Hospital Center. Gaváta giggled in her immaturity of not knowing exactly how to react. For the moment, she had no pain.

Sissy arrived shortly thereafter because Brother Holman was picking her up. All went well and after 3 ½ hours of labor, the healthy Isaiah Nehemiah Smith came forth. The first arms he was thrown in, even before his own mother, was Aunt Sissy, who eventually became known to him as Nana. After seeing the love she gave to this child, her name quickly went from Aunt Sissy to Nana, all throughout the family.

Regina came to the hospital for the next two days and loaded Isaiah's baby bag up with the hospital's baby formula, explaining that, "We mind as well make Medicaid pay for as much as possible because baby milk costs too much. On top of the fact, that these little ready-to-serve bottles can be kept at room temperature and will help you when you're tired late at night." God knows, her mother tried to do what she could while mentally grasping that her 15-year-old daughter had just given birth to a baby less than nine months after she had lost her father. How could a person even fathom sobriety and go through all of this? But somehow, in her best mind of trying to be a good grandmother, Regina mustered up a nickname for him, Mr. Dribbles.

Christian (Chrissy)

"Get down, Get down now! Put your nose to the wall! Put your hands up! Put your faces on the ground! Don't move!" were just some of the many commands that the United States Park Police yelled as they raided Regina's house at 35 Randolph Place, Northwest on March 4, 1993. Gaváta could hardly keep her nose to the wall because her stomach was so big that it met the wall first. She whimpered and cried as she watched the masked officers treat Big Carlos like a hardened criminal. The police were all upstairs in her mother's area of the home.

The warrant squad, the task force and the investigative team failed to do their research properly so that they would know that the basement had been zoned off as a separate unit and that Gaváta and Carlos was paying rent directly to the Estate of the late Bishop McCollough, her grandfather. Her mother had legal rights to the upper level as an heiress. They all later learned that the undercover narcotics officers had reported that Carlos was a big time drug dealer who supplied to the addicts who lived and frequented the upstairs. Their intel was way off. Carlos was solely dependent on what Gaváta could provide.

The next day, the couple decided to go to Prince George's Plaza Shopping Mall in Hyattsville, Maryland. Carlos decided to take back roads due to his ongoing paranoia from the raid. Not to mention, he didn't have a driver's license. Wouldn't you know it, as soon as they crossed the line from D.C. into Maryland, sirens came seemingly out of nowhere. They plotted a tale of her being in labor so that was why he HAD to drive. The Caucasian female officer said, "I'll give you both two choices, you can either get in the ambulance I've called and go to the hospital or you can get into my squad car and go to jail. I will let you park the car if you get in the ambulance, since this is a residential neighborhood. However, if I put you in my car, I will have to have yours towed." They both agreed to quickly park and they got into the ambulance taking notice of where to pick the car up from later. Female intuition told Gaváta to at least go through with the basic preliminary examination. Thank goodness she did. Within 30 minutes the officer arrived at the hospital and she stayed for a while.

"Well Ms. Smith, you've dilated 4 ½ centimeters. Your contractions are a bit strong. Don't you feel them?" asked the examining physician.

She looked at him in shock. "What?" she replied. "No Way! I don't feel a thing, My water hasn't broken." The doctors at Washington Hospital Center who had done her prenatal care through both pregnancies, had drilled in her head the importance of 'complete disclosure' and honesty with your doctor, for the sake of the baby. Knowing this, she explained to the doctor, the events of yesterday, -- all about the raid. He was able to determine that her nerves were malfunctioning and that's why she couldn't feel anything or know that she was in labor. The officer who pulled them over, was essentially a blessing. Still feeling a bit of discomfort around this medical staff, and knowing that she had to get special shots due to her RH Negative Blood, she knew that she did not want to deliver at this hospital. After much back and forth consultation with Washington Hospital Center's on- call OB/ GYN, she signed herself out and vowed to go directly there. Instead she went home, back to Randolph Place, to tell her mother the good news. She packed a bag, fixed steak and potatoes *against all medical advice*, asked the regular in-house addicts of the house to go and boost baby clothes, then stopped and picked up a couple of bags of skittles on her way. After about five misread sonograms and Carlos looking at his watch about 100 times, dying to get out the door to the nightclub, contractions finally hit hard. The medical assistant, burst her water, she went into the delivery room and gave birth to a happy, healthy daughter Christian A'Lexus Fields. Within 48 hours they were home and Regina fought every iota of the look of intoxication, trying to be there for, love on, babysit, and do things for Chrissy.

Carlos Jr. (Giz)

"You gotta be kidding me." was the exasperated notion of almost every family member of Gaváta when she went back for her six-week postpartum appointment from Christian, learning that she was pregnant again. "Girl, you are crazy, this is your senior year of high school." This was the disappointment that no one elected to mask. She was so in love with Carlos Sr. that she didn't even give her body time to heal properly. And, she paid for it. The condition was called Placenta Previa. Her placenta covered her womb instead of being in its rightful place atop. Any amount of kicking from the baby, or too much walking or activity by Gaváta, caused a massive amount of blood loss. In late September of 1993 she was placed in the hospital on bed rest in the trendelenburg position. During that time Regina was able to sneak non-hospital food to her daughter's room without the medical staff finding out. She was always so happy to see her mother, especially when she brought Apostolic United Church Kitchen food. Sometimes the visits were short in length, but her consistency in coming was appreciated.

On November 19, 1993 after an exciting visit with her mother, her boyfriend Carlos, Aunt Sissy and a few other friends and close members of the family, Gaváta began to bleed and hemorrhage enormously. One warm blanket went between her legs and an even warmer blanket laid on top of her as she was rushed into the delivery room. The last thing she remembered was an oxygen mask being placed on her face. This was an anesthesia to put her to sleep. She awoke hours later to tubes in her nose and throat, staples in her stomach, and a bright light in her face. Someone instructed her to swallow, and when she did, tubes were snatched out as she coughed. She was told that an emergency C-section had to be performed to try to preserve the life of both her and the child. As she was wheeled out, she was met by her mother, Aunt Sissy and Big Carlos. Between family and the medical staff, she was told about the one pound son that she'd just given birth to. Regina promised to be there the next day to take her to the NICU (Neonatal Intensive Care Unit). Even in an intoxicated state, although late as always, she came as promised, and wheeled her in to see her incubated newborn son. As heart wrenching as it was, Regina was there to try to comfort her baby girl as much as possible.

RéJene (Woo)

"She's lying! She's saying that she is only ten weeks. I've seen scarred tissue, but it's not that much scarred tissue in the world. That child is every bit if 16 weeks." said the medical staff of the Women's Clinic in Washington Hospital Center. Rob's girlfriend Peaches went with Gaváta to get an abortion and overheard the doctors and nurses talking about her. Peaches told Vá about the discussion she had heard, once she returned from being examined. "Dang 'P', I done sat down Mamma's house, stuck on stupid, selling drugs like I'm addicted to them, and now all these weeks have passed by and it's too late to get an abortion. All of my kids are still babies, *for real*, and Big Carlos cheats every time I turn around, so I don't know what I am going to do." exclaimed Gaváta, with all sincerity to Peaches.

As time went by, she elected to keep the baby and decided that this child would have a name honoring the two mothers in her life. RéJene would be a version of Regina and Marie would be Spanish for Mary.

September 6, 1996, while sitting in the house getting a pedicure from a girl name Trish, who was once Carlos cousin, Dan's girlfriend. But at this time, she was Gaváta and Carlos ménage a trois' lover. Contractions like she had never felt, began to consume her. They were coming too close, so she informed Carlos, went to tell her mother, called Sissy, packed a bag, and went to the hospital.

The labor room was very comfortable and had a cherry wood décor. Within six to eight hours of labor, family and friends, came and went. More than them, addicts who claimed to be immediate family, found a way, just to get in to buy drugs. Yes she sold drugs while in labor and between contractions. How sick was that? The doctors came to inform Carlos that the contractions was close enough that they wanted to administer the epidural and prepare for delivery. Because of the direction in which her last C-section was performed, she would have to deliver through cesarean again. Carlos had already made it known that he could not sit through such a procedure so he had asked Gaváta's mother to do so. Regina agreed. She held Vá's hand when they asked her to sit up and bend over while carefully putting the epidural in place. When they laid her down, giving the anesthesia time to take effect Regina left the room to go to "take a hit". Upon her return, she had to be rescrubbed for purposes of sterilization. While holding her baby girl's hand with one hand she fed Vá ice chips with the other. Somehow she was able to multitask and on look attentively at every cut, move, fold, and action of the doctors performing the surgery. When RéJene Marie Fields entered the world, within thirty seconds of her first cry, Regina said, "Now, who is gonna tie up the tubes? Where's the doctor?" The OB/GYN acknowledged who would do the additional procedure. She sat by Gaváta's side until the last stitch was put in place and when it was, she simple leaned back and said, "Whew. Sing a little song, say a little prayer, now mamma's gonna get her a breath of fresh air." That *air* was the inhalation of a pull of cocaine from a crack pipe. She left and wasn't seen for two more days. The only reason of her return at that time was because Peaches was in labor with another one of her grandchildren, Gaváta's niece, Bobby-Girl. Washington Hospital Center had dubbed the babies being born at this time as "Blizzard Babies", indicating that they were conceived during one of the worse snow storms in Washington, DC, *from November 1995 through January 1996.*

SECTION IV:

THE NEED TO KNOW

CHAPTER 13

How much really should a child be allowed to know? Is there still a such thing as 'grown folks business' or did that only apply to adults who weren't on crack?

For as long as she could remember, Gaváta was regularly informed of who her mother's drug suppliers were, the areas where she purchased her drugs from, who she was getting high with, what specific house or street in which they were using the drugs, who her mom resold them to, what men and/or women Regina was sleeping with, what type of vehicle she was likely to be riding in or driving, and who cooked the crack with what chemical. Her mother justified this disclosure by saying that if something happened to her, she wanted to make sure that someone knew who, what, when, why, and where. Some may feel that Gaváta was told way too much. Unbeknownst to many, her mother had overdosed and been given bad drugs at different points in time. There were many family events occurring of which Regina was often uninformed. Isn't it possible that there was an incessant longing her life to hear the words "I love you. How are you today?" from someone who really meant it, not from someone who was trying to manipulate and get another fix? Don't addicts long for love and acceptance too?

Words may not have been spoken, but Regina's actions towards her baby girl echoed trust, reliance, longing, assurance, and unvoiced expectations. It was as if by telling her so much and allowing her to be *in the know*, Regina anticipated that Gaváta's loyalty would be one in that she'd never be left out, or have to feel total inadequacy within the family ever again.

Taking great pride in what was commissioned to her, Gaváta likewise kept her mother *in the know*. Her duties were fulfilling and gave her the sense of the wholeness she craved within their mother daughter relationship. Until......

SECTION V:

FAREWELL DADDY

CHAPTER 14

On the cold Thursday of March 21 in 1991, Gaváta wasn't at a home. Instead she was in the 1700 Block of Lawrence Street, Northeast. While there she attempted to disclose to Teo, in her softest tone that she was pregnant with Isaiah. *At that time she thought Teo was Isaiah's father, until a startling discovery in a 2008 DNA test that revealed that his father is Michael Boone.* Teo had put a silver snub-nosed .357 revolver to her head demanding that she abort the baby because it would ruin his life. In fear, in pain, and in confusion she cried and begged for her life, by vowing to end her pregnancy. He allowed her to leave with sniffles and tears still running down her face. She caught the Metro Bus home having to transfer twice, while dealing with all of her teenage confusing emotions. Upon arrival home, she took a deep breath before knocking on the door and ringing the bell. Before her wrist could even attempt to make impact, she heard an opera-like vociferation. Aunt Sissy's wailing was accompanied by laments saying, "Uncle Walter, I told you not to do it to me. Oh! No! What am I gonna do without you Uncle Walter?" It was at this moment that she knew. It was at this moment that Gaváta was beyond convinced that her grandfather had passed away. Daddy (Bishop Walter) McCollough had died and was gone to be with the Lord. In that very instance she thought, "Oh No, Where's Momma?" She then knocked to gain entry, and Sissy tried to regain her composure while answering the door. She couldn't even make eye contact with Vá. She just opened the front door with her head hung low, keeping her sniffles to a minimal, and simply saying, "Vá, shut the door behind you." She quietly sat down and waited for Sissy to talk. She just looked at the child and said, "Well, Uncle Walter's gone on home." Gaváta sat in the far corner of the couch and wept as if the couch had warm human arms to comfort her.

Once she felt that she couldn't cry any more, she went to locate the phone number to her mother's new hang out, which was off of Benning Road, Northeast. As she searched for the number, a clutter of feelings overwhelmed her. She was grieving over her grandfather's death. Her heart was in anguish by the mere fact that Sissy was distraught. Gaváta was enraged because her mother not at the hospital with her own father in his final moments. Regina wasn't even there for her to help her sort through the events of her day. She didn't care about her mom's addiction. At this point, she just wanted her mother to know about her pregnancy, that she almost got shot today, that the baby's father is violent, and that she needed her to hold her like never before, through this bereavement and unfamiliar emotional rollercoaster.

Most of the grandchildren weren't allowed to see their grandfather, Bishop McCollough, during his stay in the hospital. She envied her cousins whose parents were diligent and on the front line pushing and making sure they were able to spend some sort of time with Granddaddy during his last days.

Gaváta located the telephone number and dialed. When someone answered, with much urgency, she asked, "Hello! Can I please speak to my mother? Is Regina there? This is her daughter Gaváta. She gave me the number." After about three or four, "Hold on, ---- Wait a minute,---- I think she's coming" replies, a belk of frustration caused her to yell, "Put my mother on the phone! My grandfather just died! Her father is dead!" Quickly the phone was passed along and Regina finally said, 'Hello."

"Granddaddy just died! You're using your breath to get high and Granddaddy just took his last breath."

"Oh my God!" was Regina's first response. She then went on to say, "Gaváta, I'm coming. Let me call someone for a ride. Where is everyone? Are they still at the hospital?"

The angry teenager said, "I don't know", slammed down the phone and ran upstairs to her room.

Regina never called back but Sissy came upstairs later, to talk to and comfort her.

CHAPTER 15

Well Granddaddy was laid to rest after several funerals up and down the East and West Coast. The very next thing on everyone's mind was the almighty dollar and how soon, what would be issued.

Not really being sure if she was instructed or if she intuitively felt it within, Regina was rushed to rehab. Gaváta went with Uncle Buddy and Sissy to carry her to this extra expensive establishment about 3 ½ hours from D.C. During the drive there, they stopped at Arby's Fast Food Restaurant for food and a restroom break. Little did they know, Regina had her get-high paraphernalia and at least one hit of crack with her. While they we were ordering, she was in the restroom getting high. Sissy went to get her, and cleverly summoned her by asking, "Regina, what do you want on your Roast Beef?" Regina said, "I'm coming Lil' Mamma." She flew out of the bathroom, rushed to the Salad & Fixing Bar, and between nervousness and intoxication, she thickly spread horseradish on her roast beef sandwich, instead of mayonnaise. They were in the car by the time she realized what she had done. Gaváta found it hilarious. The look on her mother's face when she bit into the sandwich was priceless. They were both riding side by side in the backseat. When they arrived to their destination, Regina stuffed something in the crack of the seats and instructed her daughter to throw it away as soon as they got home and not to show or tell anyone. In her nosiness, as soon as the car pulled away, Gavåta went into the crack of the seat, pulled out the wrapped cloth and unveiled Regina's lighter, stem, and other drug usage effects. She whispered to and then passed it up to Sissy. Uncle Buddy looked in Sissy's hand and literally went off. He fussed and preached about it all the way home.

Regina stayed there for about sixty to ninety days. She came home and remained clean for about a month, maybe two, just long enough to get some money.

Uncle Mutch, Uncle Buddy, and Uncle Jimmy were her three elder siblings. She was the baby and the only girl. The three of them were all issued sums ranging from $100,000 to $250,000 by that Summer. They shared some of their inheritance with their children and enjoyed their portion of the money. Sissy also got a nice little chunk from her Uncle Walter which she immediately put in a Certificate of Deposit Account.

One day while Gavåta was chillin' alone in the family's Allison Street home, mail came. A letter addressed to her Uncle Mutch, Walter McCollough Jr., looked unfamiliar to her partly because he never received mail there. She decide to take a peek, but it would be difficult because the side was perforated and required it to be torn open. She thought to herself, "Oh Well!" The notice was very short. It was four digits on a square sheet of paper stating that a bank card would arrive in seven to ten business days and to use this PIN (Personal Identification Number). For two weeks, Gavåta refused to go anywhere before the mailman came. Each day she'd feel each piece of mail waiting for the texture of hard plastic to be felt through an envelope. When it did arrive, she opened it and walked down to the New Hampshire Avenue Shopping Center to the Citizens Bank, to give this process a try. She got out $300 and saw the remaining balance on the receipt. This 15 year-old's eyes bucked open wide. This was an exhilarating moment. Was children now allowed to hit the lottery? If so, she believed that she had just hit the jackpot. Her cousins had been bragging about what they had gotten from their parents, so that was her justification. But, in actuality, she felt no remorse because according to all that she had learned, Uncle Mutch introduced Regina to crack cocaine. So in her eyes, he was the cause of her not having the mother she needed and since there was no other way of a 110 pound child getting back a 250 pound man, this would be her revenge and she'd enjoy the benefits. She called up her cousin Kimi, her partner in crime, and every day for about three months, they'd spend $300-$500 a day.

July 19, 1991 ended that fiasco. The money was depleted in totality and after a night of hard-clubbing and drinking, the love of her life, Michael Boone, had beaten her for not having sex with him, in front of his friends. Kimi had left her in the hotel with him, getting beat on, and he wound up hitting her in the head with a large pink-globed lamp. When everyone left, one of his friends stayed, as if for sex, but Gaváta drifted off to sleep through her agony and tears. The next day, she showed up at Sissy's dry cleaners in a cab, asking her to pay the fare. She was beaten and broken, physically, emotionally and psychologically. Regina was eventually notified of Gaváta's assault and all she could offer was, "I just saw him around 14th and 'R' Streets." That spoke volumes, in that she had recently been to see him for a drug buy.

With Regina's vacillating recovery habits it wasn't until 1995-1996 when she would be able to have reasonable access to her mutual fund at Putnam Investments, allowing her to do what she please with her money. Even then, Grandma Madam's name was on the account as an *attempted* form of restriction. Initially, before she was even given any financial allowance, the home that was granted to her as a segment of her father's assets, was fully remodeled and Regina was allowed to move in during the Summer of 1992. Gaváta leased the basement for her and Isaiah, paying rent directly to the estate. She even got it zoned as a separate unit, to avoid any overpowering that could take place by her mother. Ironically, as weird as the set up was, this was the first time her and her mother had ever lived in the same house without Sissy or Grandma Madam. Inwardly, Gaváta was happier than she'd ever been just to know that her mother's presence was so close.

SECTION VI:

THE BEST SPOT IN D.C.

CHAPTER 16

"Oh hell no! I won that hand. Pay me."

"Regina you did not win. I laid that Spade."

"No, you didn't."

"Yes, I did."

"Regina listen. I laid this Diamond and then she laid down this ..."

"Forget it! I don't wanna hear no more. This is my daddy's house. Pay me my house hit. Now *win* that", Regina screamed sarcastically while debating on who won the last card game. The card table was the long dining room table, which was about eighty-five inches long with two or three regular dining-room chairs on either side. But, at the head of the table, was one breakfast-bar-high chair that was exclusively for Regina, meaning that she was the only one allowed to sit there. She was the queen of her home and made sure that everyone who stepped foot inside knew that she was Queen "B". Her attitude exuded that of an only child, even though she was the baby of four and the only girl. Every addict who lived there or frequented the home, had a position. There was a door man, a look-out man inside, a look-out who stayed outside, a couple of babysitters for her grandkids, someone who washed dishes and kept the kitchen clean, others who cleaned the rest of the home, a chauffeur, someone to get her plain UTZ Potato Chips and strawberry flavored water every morning, someone to wash clothes, and both her male and female lovers who both slept in the same room with her. Sometimes the men would rotate according to their current worth. Regina beliefs and teachings of *don't do it if its not beneficial*, caused her to set her own Reginaism-Standard. That standard was that if a man became too dependent on her, he rotated into the doorman position and a more worthy man, stepped up to the plate to *try* to be the man of the house.

Between the money she had gotten from her father and her new drug connect, an eighth of kilo of crack cocaine was sold every other day out of her home on Randolph Place, Northwest. No quantity or wholesale larger than one gram was sold. Everything was sold in dimes, which are ten dollar increments. Gaváta somehow became the dealer who would take every moving dollar. She even sold $3 hits of crack. Regina charged her inflated flexible fees for selling in her home. She didn't mind because she didn't have to deal with the outside streets where the patrolling police or the stick-up boys were. So the payment was worth the 'safety'. Gaváta even went so far as naming the crew who frequented her mother's house. They were called the "Derelicts". Ironically most of them had legal jobs, a steady source of income, or was just the best at the illegal activities they committed. There was an elite crew who did heists for real expensive unique jewelry. There was a pilot, a car repair man, a car salesman, a painter, a carpenter, a cement truck worker, a cab driver, a car salesman, an eyeglass booster, check writers, a dialysis patient, preachers, singers, cooks, and even a professional cable installer, *who experienced love at first sight*, and later became her husband and my loving dad. Then there was a booster, who was able to deliver whatever was needed, whenever. He was the most sought out of all the crew.

CHAPTER 17

July 4, 1997, was Gaváta's first husband's 21st birthday. Twelve days after that, would be there third wedding anniversary. She decided to throw a lap dance party celebration for Big Carlos. Whichever of the dancers he liked best, he would be allowed to get that *one* for his private party on their anniversary. Gaváta spoke to her mother, who agreed to rent her the house for the 4th of July Birthday gala. She paid her mother in both crack cocaine and cash. Regina's motto of "Don't do it if it's not beneficial", lasted throughout her addiction. Therefore, there was more payment in cash than value to drugs. When that afternoon arrived, Vá paid her mother and Regina packed a few things and went to a hotel. The evening progressed and the party was jumping, the strippers arrived, they were paid and everything seemed to be moving along with a sense of forwardness. The announcement was made in the party, "Can all the ladies step outside please?" Gaváta had brought the women outside while the strippers did their 'set'. Big Carlos liked seeing one-on-one girl action. She didn't elect to be inside to see a bunch of horney young men, oogling and going broke. So she stayed on the front porch playing, laughing, and talking to the other female partygoers. To her surprise her mom drove up, while the highlights of the night were taking place. She said, "Hold up Ma. Women aren't in the house right now. The strippers are doing their *set*."

"Girl if you don't move out of my way. They ain't got nothing I haven't seen before." she replied.

"Ma but wait....." yet there was nothing she could say to stop her as Regina pushed and excused her way through the crowd. Within seconds, her voice resounded in a loud aggressive tone, "Oh Hell No! Yall done lost yall mind. I know yall ain't on my dining room table laying down doing... Oh No! – Vá get in here." Embarrassed, she sat on the porch with her head down. When Regina reached her room, it was evident that she thought that her daughter did not hear her call so she hung her head out of her bedroom bay window, which overshadowed the front porch and she said, "Vá, come here." Disturbed by what had just happened, but calmed because no one seemed to have been deterred from their enjoyment, she answered her mother's summons.

"Mam?" she asked, as she entered the room.

"Vá, I am really disappointed in how you've handled things. I'm not going to let you tear up my house. Then, those broads down there doing God knows what on the table we eat at. Are you crazy?"

Gaváta remained silent. Her mother then went on to say, "Okay, now give me *something* so I can go." If Regina's original reason for returning to the house was to buy more drugs from her daughter, Vá knew that right now she wouldn't get a dime and was expected to pay for her "mess up". She gave her mom more drugs and Regina left. The rest of the night went along as planned.

SECTION VII:

NEAR DEATH x2

CHAPTER 18

"Vá, Vá, Honey. Come on Moo-Moo, get up, we gotta go." Sissy gently nudged Gaváta, trying to wake her up.

With the resistance of a groggy child, she repeatedly responded. "Uh-un-noooooo." Finally sitting up, Sissy told her to get dressed because they had to go. Regina had just been rushed to the hospital. Both Gaváta and Sissy quickly dressed and hurried to the emergency room. While sitting in the waiting area, Vá worried about what was going on with her mother. What actually happened? After Sissy ran back and forth from the nurses station, to in-the-back, to the waiting room, quite a few times, she sat down next to Gaváta and said, "Well Honey, Wali stabbed your mother up pretty badly. I think that she's gonna be alright." Confusion bombarded this child's head so the words from her mouth were that if one simple request, "I want to see her. I want to see my mother." Sissy got up to go to try to get an approval because children weren't generally allowed in that restricted area. When she returned, she extended her hand for Gaváta to accept, and together they walked through the double doors of the trauma ward. As the child scanned the hallway which was lined in patients in beds which were strategically placed along the walls, she earnestly sought out her mother, while gripping Sissy's hand even more firmly. To the adult eye, the hospital's service that night screamed OVERLOAD; HIGH CAPACITY; MINIMAL STAFF; INSUFFICIENT CARE CAPABILITIES. In locating Regina's unrecognizable body, Sissy guided Gaváta over to the bed, that was midway down the hall on the left side. She looked like someone who had been made up for a gory scene out of a movie. With a weakened voice, Gaváta asked the question, "Ma? Mamma, is that you? It's me Vá." Regina turned over slightly to see her baby girl, all while letting out the pain to her every movement vocally in penetrating moans. Instantly, the child's eyes welled up in tears for she never could have been prepared to see her mother in this state of wretchedness. Dried up dark red blood was all over her face, head, hands, and visible body. Patches of hair had to be shaved to clean and suture the wounds. Swelling from the stabbing, had begun to cause facial disfiguration. This experience was mortifying for Gaváta, and much more painful emotionally, physically, mentally and spiritually for Regina. In spite of the obstacle of addiction, she always viewed her mother as *strong*. So to actually see her mother as a weakened vessel, who appeared to be at her lowest common denominator, knocking on deaths door, was incomprehensible to her young mind.

Once back at the house, Sissy sat Gaváta down to tell her that her oldest cousin, Wali, had stabbed Regina over thirty times, and that the most detrimental wound which raised the question of life or death, was a half-millimeter away from her esophagus. But why? Had Wali snapped? What had happened? Why would Wali hurt the

Aunt who had primarily raised him? This was very difficult to grasp as a real-life event. Wali apparently had been spending money all night, using crack with Regina and her beau. When his money was gone, she thought that it would be okay to pack up, and go off to a hotel to chill with her man for the rest of the evening and the early hours of the morning, off of what she had benefitted from her nephew all that night. Wali became angered, and instead of expressing that frustration argumentatively, he suppressed his true feelings, and calmly called her to the half-bath restroom in the basement of Allison Street. When she stepped inside, Wali said, "Aun't I love you." He immediately clicked the lights off, and proceeded to unsystematically mutilate her. When his mental vices allowed him to digress, he put down the knife, walked up the stairs to the main level of the house, dialed 9-1-1 and said, "Hello, my name is Walter McCollough III. I just stabbed my aunt up pretty badly so y'all might want to get an ambulance here as soon as possible. I'm not going anywhere. I'll be here waiting on the police." I believe it was at this point the family fully embraced the nick name that Wali had been giving himself for several years, "TIC" *which was short for LunaTIC*. The next night around midnight, as Gaváta sat in the house restless, she decided to call The D.C. Department of Corrections, The Lorton, Virginia Prison. She asked to speak to someone who could notify an inmate of a family emergency. She was transferred a few times and then someone finally took her call. "Yes, my name is Gaváta I am calling regarding Walter McCollough Jr. I am his niece. His son Wali, stabbed his sister, which is my mother, on last night. She is in the hospital in critical condition."

"Ok, so you said that your name is..........."

"Gaváta, Gaváta Smith and I am Walter McCollough, Jr.'s niece."

"And your mother's name is ...."

"Regina McCollough"

The Lorton Staff Member then said, "Okay, I will make sure that this information gets to Mr. McCollough. But let me ask you this. I know Mr. McCollough, so is it okay that I tell him in the morning? I don't think it would be good to wake him up with this kind of news."

"Sure. That's fine." Gaváta then thanked him and hung up the phone.

Gaváta used the time of her mother's hospitalization to bond with her by repetitive visits and sneaking her Apostolic United Church Kitchen food that she wasn't suppose to have.

Of course, Wali was arrested, but the turbulences that would occur within the family for the next few weeks, were even more drastic. The D.C. Superior Court Judge set a bond. Granddaddy, The Bishop, in his very natural fatherly love for his one and only baby girl, forbade any one to pay a dime to get Wali out of jail. Wali, Walter McCollough III, held the *family name*. He was granddaddy's descendant - a direct descendent. Granny, was a loving, motherly, nurturing God-fearing forgiving grandmother. Grandma Madam, his wife, heard the cry of her oldest son from prison, a cry for his only son, and so she went against Granddaddy's request, and bailed Wali out of jail. There were eleven noted grandchildren and seven of which were boys. Wali, Tony, and Rob often hung out together which was inevitable since Regina was a caregiver to them all at one point or another. All of the grandchildren, both male and female loved and adored Aun't, which was what they all called Regina. There was often talk of retaliation especially after Regina got out of the hospital and was nervous and frantic about the mere sight or talk of knives. One Sunday, about two years after the tragedy, Uncle Buddy preached a sermon and the spirit was moving extremely heavy in church. Wali was there and a compelling hovering of forgiveness encamped the room. After Regina hugged and reluctantly forgave Wali, the fellas of the family seemingly followed suit. *Healing* was knocking at the door of everyone's heart, but The McCollough Family realized that this was a process that would take time. Regina was still fearful of both Wali and knives and had no problem admitting it.

CHAPTER 19

"Bam, bam, bam", "Come on Gaváta open the door !!!" These were the sounds of the banging and shouting at Vá's front door. She had run out of crack to sell and was annoyed by all of the loud shouting and constant harassment of her drug clientele. "What is it?" she replied. Someone yelled, "They need you at the corner. Your mother was in an accident. They're rushing her to the hospital." By the time she got to the corner, every possible named emergency vehicle was on North Capitol Street, Northwest between Randolph and 'R'. The police wouldn't let her through and she had only been advised that her mother had already been rushed from the scene. Upon arrival at the hospital, Gaváta quickly found the group of family and friends that were there for her mom. Everyone was standing outside of a trauma / x-ray / emergency surgery room. One hour turned into two hours. Two hours turned into three hours. And, three hours turned into almost four hours. Finally, someone came out and said that things didn't look good, she had been damaged severely, that an emergency surgery was being performed, skin grafts would need to be done and that several medical procedures would be performed over the next couple of weeks, but that her getting through the next 48 hours was critical. It was like déjà vu. Hugs were given. Many tears were shed. Sorrow, grief and pain encamped the family. During the next couple of hours, the atmosphere was very solemn. Uncle Mutch came in and asked, "What happened to what she had on her?" He went on to explain, "She had just went to cop [drugs] and she was on her way back so who got that? The police didn't find it so, where is her property and all the stuff she had?" Everyone looked at him with much disdain. After about another two hours, the medical team came out exhausted and drained.

"What is going on? Why are they over there whispering? Why are the doctors just talking to the older adults? I'm grown too. I wanna know what the hell is up with my mom. Did she die? I don't like the looks on everyone's faces." Gaváta thoughts were running rampant. "Oh now, for real? Are you serious? Are they really gonna stand over there and have a side bar conversation like we're not sitting right here? Maybe if I eavesdrop and listen real hard..... Did they just say her ribs are broken? Something about her pelvis? What the??? ----- Wait, now here comes the doctors again. What is going on? Okay now everyone is saying 'whew' and grabbing their chest in a sigh of relief. Here they come."

"Come on yall. Your mother is already upstairs in a room. That was the girl Loraine that was riding in the car with Regina." said Uncle Mutch.

The ride upstairs to the Intensive Care seemed like an eternity. Aunt Sissy had to get stern with the medical staff to bend the rules about 'no children allowed', especially at that hour of the night. Gaváta hid behind Sissy a little, fearful of what she was going to see, even at this big-girl age. What she saw broke her heart. Once again Regina was frail, full of stitches and dry blood, and holding on for dear life.

Over time, day by day, she got better and began to regain her strength. She had adopted Loraine as her sister because this unified struggle of healing brought them very close together.

Later the family learned the details of the accident. While Regina was coming back from copping drugs, she attempted to make a left turn onto her street. She was driving a blue convertible Geo Storm. She was blind-sighted due to the tunnel and underpass on North Capitol Street, so as she was turning, a Nissan 300zx was speeding in excess of 75mph, in a 25mph zone, and spiraled the car she was driving out of control. Regina and Loraine's bodies ejected to opposite ends of the block. Regina landed on North Capitol and 'R', on the steps of a church and Loraine landed on North Capitol and Randolph, on the steps of a funeral home.

Later in life after getting clean, Loraine died of AIDS, but will always be dear to the family as the sister Regina was blessed in life to finally have.

SECTION VIII:
LET THE CRIMES BEGIN

CHAPTER 20

In efforts of being a responsible new teenage mother, who could save and manage funds properly, Gaváta opened a new bank account at Crestar Bank. Before long, the desire for materialism sank in. She began to write checks. She learned that check authorization systems didn't have access to the actual information about fund availability. Isaiah, even as a baby, began to have any designer name brand imaginable as long as it could be purchased from Hecht's, Nordstrom, Foot Locker, Woodward & Lothrop, or Macys. Soon, a *dare-like-adrenalin* engulfed her. She began to try everything from grocery and electronics to furniture stores. Some were successful and others weren't . This began her on an irreversible life of crime that would ruin many years of her future. While drug were never her addiction, checks, shopping and money became a compulsive vice that she could not control. When the bills were due she resulted to checks. When depression overwhelmed her, she resulted to checks. When relationship difficulties arose and the feeling of competing with other women for fear of losing her mate, came to surface, she relied on checks to buy love, friendship and to make her into the person that she felt that she needed to be, in order to elude loneliness or abandonment. She embezzled an excess of $95,000 from MCI in counterfeit business checks. She even began to purchase car transmissions, postage stamps, laptops, projectors, high-end cameras and all sort of electronics, and sell them for cash. She became a supplier of these items for many vendors and merchants.

Neither Sissy nor Regina tried to steer Gaváta from this criminal behavior. Instead, when Gaváta felt the need for bonding time with her mother, she would invite her to get her hair or nails done. When she wanted to express a token of love for Sissy, she'd buy her some shoes, boots, or jewelry, that she never wore. [Which Vá believed was Sissy's unique way of not sanctioning what she was involved in.]

> *Never did she think as a young adult, that this life of criminal behavior would eventually lead to her long term imprisonment and losing three husbands, missing her children's major events in life, graduations, giving birth to their children (Gaváta's grandchildren), the death of her own grandmother, Grandma Madam, and so many more of life's one-time occasions.*

SECTION IX:

YOU'RE MY MOM SO I WILL NOT MAKE YOU FEEL EXILED

CHAPTER 21

———◆———

July 16, 1994, the wedding was scheduled for 12pm. Gaváta and
Carlos was eighteen years old and would be getting married at New
Bethel Baptist Church on 9th and S Streets, NW. This was the church
across the street from Sissy's Dry Cleaners. She had asked Uncle
Buddy to officiate her wedding at the Apostolic United Church.
But, because Carlos wasn't a member, he respectfully declined. Elder
Aquilla Moxely, a Reverend who was referred to them by Teo's mother,
from Greater Mt. Calvary Holy Church would preside in adminis-
tering the vows. Teo's mother was always so loving no matter the situation or circumstances. She was and still is a committed woman of
God and member of Greater Mt. Calvary Holy Church where Gaváta
would eventually join in January 2018.

The wedding was a "go". The plan was for Gaváta to pay her regular hairdresser, Anthony, a stylist from Sandra and The Stars on 14th
and T Streets, NW, to do the hair of all 12 females of her wedding
party including Regina. He was going to come in at 6am the day of
the wedding, to begin. Gaváta would get her hair done last since the
wedding couldn't start without her. She had also paid a team from

Mary Kay to come and do appropriate fitting makeup, so that the women wouldn't look like Las Vegas drag-queens. Everyone was in place in the church at 2pm when Gaváta finally arrived *late*. To be so organized, she had forgotten everything. She even left her panties and stockings at the house. So, while it was easy for her to find a cheap pair of pantyhose, she wore them up under an eloquently embroidered white gown detailed by a variety of white beading, with no panties on. The father who was on her birth certificate, Bobby Smith Sr., was there to give her away. Her favorite brother Tony, was there and his Uncle Vick sung for them. Her Aunt Rozena sang as well. The children began to tire as their shoes started hurting her feet. Regina was present with bells on. In spite of her mouth being twisted, her face flaking, and half nodded out, Gaváta was just happy to have the presence of her mother in her immediate view.

The reception was held at the Howard University Hotel on Georgia Avenue, Northwest. The dancing, drinking and partying was underway. But, all of a sudden, this grand idea came to the mind of Gaváta for 'an open bar'. She told her mother. Regina immediately went to the bar to make it happen and convinced them to accept her check as payment. The check was drawn on a closed bank account. Yet, the bar was open, so all the guests were happy. Dan, Carlos cousin and best man, brought Gaváta a drink that she had never tried before. It was an Amaretto Sour. Instantly, she was hooked and excessively drank them all evening long. When it came time for the toast, first Daniel gave a heartfelt speech. Then Gaváta's best friend from High School, Mary, who was their match-maker, took the microphone and gave her spiel. Lastly, Regina took the míc and the final toast was done by her.

She boldly raised her glass of Kahlua and said, "If I had a dog who could piss enough, and piss enough of this good stuff, I'd tie his legs to the top of my bed and suck his *¿!# until he drops dead, but only if I had a dog who could piss enough of this good stuff." Everyone's mouth was wide open in shock, and eventually laughter erupted and filled the banquet hall.

CHAPTER 22

———◆———

"Carlos, listen. I got a move I can make. Don't you wanna go to Disney World? I wanna take momma away from here for a minute. She still got money from the last lump sum Granny gave them, so we really won't be carrying her weight. OK?" Gaváta anxiously awaited her husband's approval.

"I'm cool with that Vá, do what you gotta do." he replied.

"Ma, I want to take you and Jiamé on your Honeymoon. Yall got married and haven't gone anywhere so my wedding gift to you all will be taking yall to Disney World." She confronted her mother with this proposition. Regina accepted and was excited. This turned out to be a couples retreat. Regina & Jiamé, Gaváta & Carlos, and Rob & Peaches.

Rushing on the plane with extreme enthusiasm, Gaváta grabbed her mother's belongings. After reaching their destination, Regina laughed while telling her to stop being so fast because all of her drugs and paraphernalia was in those bags and that they were wrapped up in aluminum foil and securely packaged. Gaváta couldn't believe it. She could have went to jail for a long time, coming through an airport with that sort of stuff on her. Oh my goodness! *Luckily this was way before 9-11.*

The vacation continued as scheduled and eventually their drugs depleted. Regina and Jiamé was determined to find more. The other two couples had planned to spend their morning, after breakfast, off site, in Kissimmee, Florida at the gun range. Regina and Jiamé came along for the ride. While the young couples were firing away, the honeymooners went to the Hardees, which was in the same strip mall. Jiamé was in the bathroom and apparently had some male bonding with a guy seemingly in his early 20's, in the bathroom. Talking almost in a mumble but speaking as quickly as possible, he patted his feet rapidly and said, "Regina, I think we got our man. He's coming out the bathroom now." A young country looking guy emerged. He and Jiamé whispered a little, and everyone was gathered, being told that it was time to go. They had to hurry and follow this car as instructed. Their new connect lead them in to the belly of a nearby city on the outskirts of Kissimmee. They were told to stay parked in a school parking lot. For about thirty minutes, the dealer was out of eye's view. Tension and paranoia were high while everyone sat silently in the minivan. The music had even been turned completely off. Tourists? In an unfamiliar drug area? Robbery? Murder? All of these thoughts and feelings went throughout the vehicle as everyone sat anxiously waiting. Finally, the guy was coming back. Things went along smoothly and the transaction was complete. The afternoon was topped off with everyone returning to the hotel and preparing to go to the dinner show, *Royal Knights*. It was to start at 7:00pm and Gaváta wanted a good seat. At 6:45pm, after much frustration during the day, Regina and Jiamé had not yet exited their rooms. Gaváta went to their room to check on them and what she saw terribly frightened her. Regina lips were so tight, she could hardly speak. Her eyes were dilated and bulging. She was trying to tell them that Jiamé didn't feel good and that they wouldn't be going. Regina is a motor-mouth so for her to be in a state where she couldn't speak, was beyond scary. Jiamé sat nearby on the edge of the bed, staring in space, not saying a word, with eyes wider than Regina, but feet moving faster than the penguin in the movie *Happy Feet*. They were both 'stuck'. Gaváta called home and talked to Ruth, her older sister. She told her all that she had seen that that Mamma looked like she was overdosing and about to die. Ruth assured her little sister that their mother would be fine and that the cocaine in Florida is much more pure than the cocaine in DC, so their reaction to it was expected and normal. Gaváta calmed down and in the days leading up to their departure, their Florida drug supplier regularly came back and forth to the hotel. Regina got a nice amount to bring back to DC to share with her friends. She even brought back some to sell. The vacation came to an end after ten days so they boarded the plane leaving the beautiful sun beaming. They left the ninety degree weather that morning and upon returning home that afternoon there was an excess of five feet of snow on the ground with flurries still falling. Home sweet home.

SECTION X:

TOO CRAZY TO BE FUNNY

CHAPTER 23

---•---

It was the funeral of Uncle Boss, Bishop McCollough's brother. During this time, all of Granny's children, with the exception of Uncle Buddy, was heavily into their active addictions. However, every family member, be they saint or sinner, knew that they had better show up for this service. It was an unspoken, uncompromising of expectations for that day.

The funeral had begun, all close family and friends were in attendance, and Gaváta sat next to her favorite cousin Kimi. They were never supposed to sit this close together in church because they always laughed, talked and played. But everyone was in such a grievous state that no one payed them any attention.

The service was at a climax. The brass trombone, symbol, and percussion bands played gospel music loudly. People stood up, clapped, shouted, cried, and rejoiced over the life of the first James "Uncle Boss" McCollough. Veering their eyes to the right, the cousins looked over and saw Regina on the right side of the church with a skin-back tambourine. She was beating it like her life depended on it, while twisting her mouth, squirming her body, yet bopping to the beat. As she got more excited her tongue moved within her inner lips causing her to display all sorts of interesting faces. Looking up further, was uncle Jimmy, the second James McCollough. He was on the choir stand to the right of the pulpit. The pulpit in The Apostolic United Church is called "The Holy Mountain", therefore, for Apostolic United Church goers, it is in-short, entitled, "The Mountain". Anyway Uncle Jimmy had his guitar and he too had an oscillating body movement. Sometimes the rotation of his slim frame would actually revolve circularly. He plucked away at the strings to the same tunes that Regina was beating her tambourine to. His mouth likewise took on a variety of strange forms. Even-more-so, due to his extreme usage of crack cocaine, his weight loss was drastic. His jaws were sank in, which interfered with his dentures fitting properly. Therefore, in his excitement as he played his instrument, his tongue not only chased the numbness and taste of cocaine in his mouth, but his tongue also had to catch his dentures every time they slid out or tried to eject themselves from his mouth. From nose to chin, it was like watching a skeletal portrayal of a dental deformation in full motion. At the front of the church on the opposite side of his siblings, but standing before the musicians, was Uncle Mutch. He was and still is a singer. His way of singing is that of preaching and grinding in voice. So over all of this noise and music, no one on any microphone or otherwise could be heard, yet Uncle Mutch stood there singing hard. On clip-art, such face could have been replaced with that of someone being constipated and longing for a bowel movement. Certain notes, caused his mouth to twist, making his lip emulate a temporary state of Belpalsy.

This was the most hilarious funeral that Gaváta and / or the McCollough family had ever experienced.

CHAPTER 24

"Vá, listen baby the drug game is all about size and them flavors."

"Well Ma, I am cooking my own stuff now and using Hennessy in the cook. I heard that when I do that it puts a nice flavor and *head* on it. Druscilla, the crack – head-lady next door, showed me how to sprinkle ashes on the cook at the end, to turn it into some nice hard, white popcorn coke."

"Yea, that may work but let Mamma show you something. Now this is called the flip." Regina had removed the glass stem from side of the crack pipe that she smoke off of. After blowing it cool, and inspecting it thoroughly she looked into the opposite side of it. She ran a piece of metal through it which resembled a straightened hook of a metal coat hanger. She got a mirror, and then she pushed it through onto the glass. Out spewed the dirty chore-boy which had been packed in it and all sorts of brown dust. Regina got a razor and scrapped all of the soot together. Her mouth twisted around and around as she bounced back and forth analyzing what she had in front of her. She then said to Gaváta, "Now you see that. That's the best part of the hit. Now you take this, and add a little bit of grain to it." She was speaking of grain alcohol. "Ooop, not too much!" Her eyes seemed to be extra wider in anticipation of the high and taste that was to come. "Now you light fire to that *billy*, and smoke that, and that is that *straight butter*." Regina grabbed her pocket size torch also known as a butane refill, and set fire to the big mirror which held her flip that was saturated in grain alcohol. No circus on earth provided such live close up entertainment. This mirror sat on Regina's bed, with flames bellowing and not an iota of fear was anywhere in the room. When the fire subdued, Regina scraped the mirror clean, reattached her stem to her crack-smoking-bowl, put strawberry flavored water in the bowl of it, placed a substantial amount of crack on the tip for her enjoyment, inserted fresh chore-boy, and waved the torch along the bottom of her pipe. The clouds rolled, she strongly inhaled, and according to her, this was the best part of it all. When she's finish and satisfied with her last act, she'd get up off of the bed, bounce around and say something like, "If you can Woo-woo, I can Woo-woo, and we can all Woo-woo-woo."

SECTION XI:

HER AH-HA MOMENTS

CHAPTER 25

There were times when Regina would have a sense of morality and civility even in the midst of her addiction.

One day out of the blue, she called Gaváta from the basement and asked her to hurry up stairs because she needed to talk to her. She went and when she reached the main level of "35, called out for her mother. *("35" was the shortened name for Regina's house located at 35 Randolph Place)* She was instructed to wait in the living room and she'd be down the steps "in a minute".

"Vá, okay now sit in this chair, and turn around." Regina instructed her keeping one hand behind her back. As her mother moved close to the chair, she then told her to close her eyes and began her sentiments.

"There is something that every little girl should have. She should get them from her mother. I want you to know that even though I am not perfect, I want to be the one to give you this." Her mom put a strand of ivory pearls around her neck. "Ok now open your eyes." Gaváta touched her neck and rubbed a few of the pearls which laid on the front part of her neck. "Thank you Ma." She rushed to the nearest mirror to see her new gift. It was so nice. As she continued to stare at her reflection, her mom kissed her cheek and left the room. Somewhere in Gaváta's mind, she remembered that on a movie, they said that if you bite on a pearl, it shouldn't break and the whiting of it should not peel. So guess what? She did just that. But when she did, the first layer of the pearl peeled away. Though a little disappointed, she charged it to the fact that her mom couldn't afford to buy real ones in the condition that she was in. She told no one about her discovery, but wore them with much pride and appreciation.

There were other times when Regina would just feel the need to be surrounded by the love of her children and grandchildren.

At about 2 a.m. while sleeping at her home in Prince Georges County, the phone rang and rang and rang. Finally Gaváta answered groggily. "Hello"

"Hey Vá, I need you all to come over here as soon as possible.

"Now, Ma?"

"Yes, Now!"

She woke her husband and children, all of who were dressed in their night clothes, and told them that they had to get up to go to "35". Unbeknownst to Gaváta, similar calls were being made to all of her siblings. Simultaneously they arrived with their sleepy children and angry spouses, in tow. When they reached the front door, you could smell the aroma of soul food. The door was rarely locked, so upon entry, in immediate view, was Regina preparing what seemed like a Thanksgiving Dinner. She gave a three minute speech of wanting to see and be with the ones she love and how family is so important. After momentary frustration of disbelief, everyone was hungry so eating was an excellent idea and the perfect offering of forgiveness. This became a sporadic welcoming event.

SECTION XII:

WHEN SHE DID GOOD

CHAPTER 26

As an English Major and a seasoned Switchboard Operator, Regina had an awesome skill set to embark on a top-notch professional career. Believe it or not, in the Eighties she worked for several elite Five Star Hotels in the D.C. Area, as a switchboard operator. In her addiction, she often chastised and fussed about the mispronunciation of words. Sometime it seemed like her hearing abilities were magnified when she was high. However, her sternness of proper speech, took root and remained imbedded in her children's lives in spite of her addiction. She told them things like ....

"You are beautiful, you don't need make up or eyeliner. I didn't make no ugly children. When you get older, what will you wear to enhance your beauty? That make up will make you look old before your time."

"Get your education. You're gonna need it. It will take you a long way."

"In your relationships, keep'em happy because what you don't do, the next woman will."

"Don't do it if it's not beneficial."

"Blood is thicker than water, but cum is thicker than blood. A person will turn on their own momma for the person that's making them cum. Now don't get it twisted, if someone is whoopin' on you, Oh, I'm coming to get what's mine, and I will listen to you whine, but don't ask me to get in the middle of your relationship cuz yall won't make up a week later and then talk about me like a dog."

A collaboration of Regina's wisdom that was instilled in her from her mother and the precious gift of maternal instinct, allowed her to *mother* even when she wasn't operating in total sanity due to her addiction. These teachings helped and guided her children into their adult lives. These words have veered them from much unhealthiness and encouraged them in what they needed to do in many situations.

SECTION XIII:

SUNDAY'S BEST

CHAPTER 27

"Up! Up! Up! It's 12:01a.m. and yall know what time it is. Ain't no drug smoking in here until 7pm." Regina announced. Somehow in Regina's mind, on Sunday she *"Remembered the Sabbath"* and tried to keep it Holy, as best as possible. That meant, that there would be no crack smoking in her house after 12:01a.m. on Saturday nights, except for her.

Sunday morning would come around and Regina would be as slow as ever. She'd blast the song, "The Potter Want's to Put You Back Together Again" by Tramaine Hawkins and sing it to the top of her lungs while getting dressed. The harder she sang, the more her mouth would twist. Every note would be off key because Regina, just *can-not-sing*. She'd throw her head back, sometimes being careless causing a run in her grey-midst or off-black stockings, but there was such passion into what she sang as if it were are prayer. Being almost ready, she'd holler downstairs and say, "I'm almost ready and I'm clearing house when I leave out. Everybody better be ready to go to church. We can smoke all night so, y'all better know how to get up Sunday Mornings and thank God for not letting nothing happen to you all week. If you ain't going to church with me, don't come back in here tonight."

Everybody in "35" would be scrambling to get clothes together to wear. Regina would dress them in whatever she could find, both the men and the women.

Gaváta, Aunt Maude, sometime Sissy, and other family would be sitting in Marshall Heights Apostolic United Church while Uncle Buddy would be preaching. Uncle Buddy could preach. Anointed! Powerful! Effective! But he would preach for hours. He'd make sure that everyone was saved and delivered from something before he ended service. He had no sympathy for Football Sundays. That did not matter to him. Souls did. With Sunday School starting at 9:00 a.m. and then service beginning at 11:00 a.m. the hour was always far spent before the benediction. At about 1:30 pm when we all thought that Uncle Buddy was done, here comes Regina and her entourage. They all looked like thrift store models with clothes too big, postures out of wack, mouths twisted, but each trying to look as dignified and sober as possible. When Uncle Buddy would see them, a burst of energy would revitalize him and a new sermon would start all over again. He'd balk out a scripture in his most grinding preaching voice like, "KNOW YE NOT THAT YOUR BODIES ARE THE LIVING TEMPLES OF GOD. WHATEVER YOU ARE DOING WITH YOUR BODY, YOU ARE DOING IT WITH GOD." The tears would start to roll and then he'd preach a little more, but a little harder. Mamma would keep on her game face being very nonchalant as if to say, "I don't know who he's referring to but he ain't talking to me." Then he'd go on and say something like, "If you know that you are not living for God. If you've brought things in this House of God that are not *of* God, come lay it on the alter right now." The crackheads would get up and the alter would be filled with pipes, stems, butane refills, chore boy, pushers and every other type of crack paraphernalia you could imagine. Regina would say, "Now look at them dummies. The liquor store and the record stores that got that stuff is closed on Sundays and I don't let nobody smoke out of my pipe. As soon as they get outta here they gonna be looking for a hit so I guess they'll be using soda cans today. I hate the way that it smells when they smoke out of cans." When it was all over and the shouting music would be coming to an end, Regina would creep to her mother's side, and whisper some sort of lie to get money. Grandma Madam, being the lady at all times, would put a smile on her face and go in her handbag, ball up some money and slip it to Regina on the side as if the whole congregation didn't know why she was up front and in her mother's ear with her coat on and all of her belongings. After getting her money, she'd nod to her crew and mouth, "Let's go." The Derelicts would leave out the regular front door of the church and Regina would leave out of the side door connected to the alter by where Madam sat. Back in the car again, fussing about the emotions that made them surrender all of their get-high material, they'd be on their way to "35".

SECTION XIV:
THE CAMOUFLAGED RECOVERY

CHAPTER 28

On October 31, 1990, during the Annual Revival at The First United Apostolic Church, Charlotte Mission edifice, Gaváta gave her life to Christ and was saved. At the point of her being given the microphone for testimony she said to everyone listening, "So the reason it has taken me so long to get saved is because I was raised off of the Ten Commandments and I just can't understand the commandment that says that I have to 'Honor my mother and my father'. How can you honor a mother like mine and how can you honor a father and you don't really know who he is?" The sanctuary echoed with silence and then the blaring sounds of the brass band struck up the loudest tune one could ever imagine. There wasn't a dry eye in the building and all who were over age forty-five were shouting mightily as if Jesus himself had descended in the midst. Gaváta just stood there in utter amazement and trying to figure out what had just occurred. When she retreated to the dining area of the church a little later, many of the older adults whispered secretly, yet scandalously to let Gaváta know that her father was a preacher down in North Carolina by the name of Miles Kilchrist. They told her how her mother had cheated on her father, Bobby Smith, Sr. and how she was the reason for their breakup. As this child started to add up the pieces, she began to recall her mother celebrating her divorce from Big Bobby and how those number of years always matched her birthdate. It all made sense. When Gaváta confronted Sissy and Aunt Molly the next day, no one would or could answer her.

Regina went to rehab again in 1991, this time it was because Granddaddy had died. It wasn't known if she went to secure her portion of inheritance or if she went because her father cried out for his *baby girl* while lying on his death bed. But one day she called home and Gaváta answered happily and said, "Ma, I got something to tell you." Regina replied, "Yeah" to instruct her to continue on, and so she went on to say, "Ma, I'm pregnant." Her mother screamed to the top of her lungs and dropped the phone. Only the sound of the phone banging against the bottom of the booth could be heard as she kept saying, "Ma. Ma. Ma." Finally, a fellow recoveree answered and asked if she was Regina's 15 year old baby girl, what had happened and if she could have her mother to call back later. Of course, Gaváta was okay with it and left it at that. Regina returned home and at some-point and relapsed yet again. But after this particular rehab journey, she had left all of her papers in the living room from the written activities that she had done in the program. One paper asked her to detail some of her secrets, and there it read for her own eyes to see, "My baby girl is not by my husband." Gaváta's heart was broken all over again but she finally knew the truth. She saw it in her mother's handwriting. Regina had gone on another binge so confronting her would be out of the question for another however-many-years. She'd wait patiently until the next time when Regina could get no money from her father's estate unless she was clean, and once again have to fake the whole rehab / recovery thing and then maybe she could talk to her soberly.

SECTION XV:

THE NINTH STEP

The ninth step of recovery says, "Make direct amends to people wherever possible, except when doing so would injure them or others."

REGINA WAS READY TO GET IT RIGHT
(Oh! Happy Day !!!!!)

CHAPTER 29

———————•———————

It was December 11, 1999, when the doors of 35 Randolph Place, Northwest was kicked in and a collaborated task force of The DC Metropolitan Police and the U.S. Park Police raided Regina's home for the last and final time.

Gaváta was serving time in Virginia State Prison and waiting to be transferred to Bryan, Texas to complete her Federal Sentence. Sissy had been diagnosed with cancer and it was spreading rapidly throughout her body as she underwent chemotherapy, radiation and drastic surgeries. But they concealed this and it hurt like hell when she found out and in the manner she found out. Gaváta's family life seemed completely topsy-turvy. Sissy was the primary caregiver of Gaváta's children, due to her incarceration. But somehow Grandma Madam and Regina would have to find a way to make provisions for them. Lil' Carlos and Chrissy could go to Virginia with Big Carlos mother and would be fine there. But Isaiah was Sissy's heart and soul. Woo *(Re'Jene's nickname)* was merely a baby.

Regina sat in the D.C. Department of Corrections while waiting for her bed space at the local female half-way house. Eventually, Regina's time came for her to be transferred to The Fairview Halfway House and she went through that process gracefully. She remained in total compliance and drug free. Her outlet was at a place called EFFORTS. The acronym stood for Employment for Former Offenders Receiving Treatment Services. As she continued to follow the rules, she was afforded the privilege of being able to periodically stop by Grandma Madam's house on her lunch breaks and of course Grandma Madam was elated to see her baby girl in such a healthy place in life.

Gaváta was steadily calling Sissy at her Dry Cleaners every morning which was her regiment, because no one had told her to do anything differently. The last time she had spoken with Sissy, she had told Gaváta that she had to go to the doctor that Tuesday because her blood pressure had dropped profusely. Gaváta knew it was very serious because Sissy did not do doctors at all. After eight to ten days of continuous calling, and not getting an answer, Gaváta became tired of the vagueness she was receiving from calling Allison Street / Granny's house. So, she decided to call the one person whom she knew in the family that would speak to her like an adult and who always seemed to stand for God and what was right, not the genre of the Apostolic United Church and McCollough Family cover-ups. She called her Aunt Maude, Uncle Buddy's wife. Gaváta simply asked, "Aunt Maude, How is Sissy?" Her reply was completely clear and honest. "Gaváta we don't know nothing too much yet. We are still waiting. They just did the surgery two days ago." Taken aback a little, Gaváta pretended to be *in-the-know* prompting on questions, "So what exactly did they have to do?" Aunt Maude went on to say, "They had to remove her kidney, her liver, and her spleen, and they put in a colostomy bag." Gaváta ended the conversation with a simple, "OK. Thank you. I love you. I will call in a few days to find out more." She went in her room and cried like a dagger had been driven into her heart. Her only comfort was that of Kirk Franklin's song, "Lean on Me". She sang it over and over as if she needed God to understand that she needed his shoulder in that moment for her to lean on. She screamed it to the top of her lungs and she didn't hear and answer, which hurt even more. A few more days went by and Gaváta was transferred out before she could call Aunt Maude again or even speak with her mother. But when she got to her new prison in Bryan, Texas, she was allowed phone calls. She called Regina and told her how she felt. She reminded her of how hurtful it was to be kept out of the loop when things were occurring with Daddy McCollough. She questioned her mother and reminded her that Sissy had in fact been her nurturing mother and why would she think that it was okay to withhold that sort of information. Again, Regina handled the situation lovingly and gracefully, allowing Gaváta the right to feel what she felt. Regina stayed on her straight and narrow path of sobriety and compliance with the halfway house, EFFORTS, and the court system, and things were really beginning to look up for her.

EFFORTS conducted N/A and A/A Meetings, Employment Readiness Courses, One-on-One Personal and Career Counseling, and all sorts of other services. They were a small organization but really gave a family-feel to all who came in and became clients. Regina quickly became acquainted with both the staff and the director, who was also a Christian. This not only gave her favor in them making extra efforts to find her employment, they referred her to a workshop at Howard University for training and to receive her Drug Addiction Counselor Certification. From there Regina began to work at major corporate employment firms up and down the 'K' Street / Connecticut Avenue Corridors of Northwest, Washington and surprisingly learned Microsoft Office Applications without much effort. She even bragged about her proficiency in Microsoft Excel, an application Gaváta, the computer guru, herself had not even fully mastered at that time. For someone who has been technically dormant for over fifteen years, this was extremely impressive. Regina began to send Gaváta money in prison and assume primary responsibility of RéJene, placing her in an expensive daycare, near her job, and even paying the tuition out of her own pocket. This was a change that was beyond comprehension.

While in prison, of course Gaváta was happy for the financial support and being able to readily talk to her mother like never before, but things were odd because she couldn't make regular everyday contact with Sissy like she was used to doing.

CHAPTER 30

Through the Chaplain's Office in FPC Bryan, Gaváta would call the hospice center where Sissy was being kept just to talk to her. And, as much as the family wanted Gaváta to believe that Sissy has lost her mind and that the chemo was causing severe Alzheimer's, Gaváta was convinced that Sissy elected to know what and whom she wanted to know. Sissy would talk to her about Isaiah, his schooling, his clothes being cleaned and how he was doing when she last saw him. She would tell Gaváta how no one would come to get her to take her out for simple rides. She would cry and complain that she couldn't believe how all that she had done for Regina, the many guns she prevented from being at her head, and the many butt whoopings she prevented her from getting, how could Regina abandon her and not spend a little time just to take her out. She would urge Gaváta that upon her release, don't deal with Regina or her Grandmother because they were not to be trusted. Gaváta would listen knowing that as long as Sissy was being her feisty fussy self, she was fine. But, many of her words took root and Gaváta would be cautious as she dealt with these people when she got out, because in her eyes, Sissy's words were the *law*.

On the cold misty day of March 5, 2001, while plucking weeds from between rocks in her landscaping job at the prison, Chaplain Wattanabe walked up to Gaváta's side and looked into the sky and said, "Isn't it a beautiful day outside Gaváta?" She knew. He invited her to come and take a walk with him. They walked back to the Chapel and went into his office. On his desk, Gaváta immediately saw the page entitled, 'Inmate Death Notice'. She fell onto the floor and wailed. To her surprise, she was being picked up and cradled by her Choir Director. The Chaplain's condolences seemed so insensitive at the time. He said, "Gaváta well you know that the Apostle Paul said, 'to die is gain', She is in a better place where she won't suffer any more." In that moment, Gaváta thought, "What the hell does the Apostle Paul know about my Aunt Sissy? That was my mother. Furthermore, I would be home July 9. Why couldn't she wait four months before she left me?" The Chaplain went on to offer Gaváta a call home. When she called home, her mother and grandmother spoke to her to comfort her as best as possible. It was her conversation and encounter with Isaiah that she dreaded because Sissy had mothered him, even more than she had mothered her. Isaiah's words were excruciating and painful. They were words, no mother could ever forget. What he said to Gaváta that day, will remain etched in her heart forever. He said, "Ma, I'm not mad at my father because he's locked up. He's been locked up so I understand that. And I am not even mad at you for being locked up because I know you was just trying to pay the bills and stuff. But I am so mad at Nana *(Isaiah's name for Sissy)* cuz she didn't have to diiiiiieeeeeeee !!!!!!!!!!!!!" He piercingly shrieked and cried the word 'die' as if someone was amputating a limb from him while he was wide awake with no anesthesia.

The memorial service arrangements went underway and everyone was pressured. Regina was in her first sober family function in over twenty years and trying to prove her trustworthiness. Everyone was trying to lend a helping hand with both the kids and the funeral. Sometimes things were said in those under-pressure moments that were hurtful and shouldn't have been said. During this time, Gaváta called Isaiah to check on him, and he was at his Grandma Star's house. He shared with his mother that his Grandma Regina had said to him, "Listen Isaiah, you done worried Sissy to death and killed her, you won't kill my Momma." Gaváta called Regina and really gave her a piece of her mind about saying such a thing not only to a child, but to *her* child. After that encounter, she was more careful with her words. The funeral came and went and Regina became RéJene 's primary caregiver.

CHAPTER 31

July 9, 2001, Gaváta came home from Federal Prison and moved in with her Grandmother on Allison Street. Regina rented a place a half-block away in an apartment building that could be seen from Granny's bedroom window. Regina lived in Granny's house eighty percent of the time too. Rob hadn't been too long come home from prison either. He was staying in Regina's apartment so there was no way that Gaváta would have ever spent one night there with him alone. He used to be so handsome but somewhere in his penitentiary journeys, he'd become addicted to drugs too. Heroine had overtaken his appearance and he had massive teeth lost. This was yet another family change that Gaváta would have never expected. Regina was now sober so to see her functioning in everyday life was so weird. Not being able to call Sissy all throughout the day for advice and just to hear her voice was uncomfortable. Sissy wasn't there to help her get on her feet and for her to go and chill in her drycleaners just to kick back and talk. Regina was fat, healthy and beautiful. Gaváta embraced her mother with both caution and a long-awaited yearning. She helped her mother send her first email and to learn how to drag & drop her first attachment in a message. Those times were fun and rememberable. They would hang at granny's, then go shopping, and Vá would watch her mother do-the-right-thing with money. They'd eat all day. So Gaváta had to stop, and take a step back and say, "OK, what is this N/A thing really about that has Regina clean after twenty-four years?" So she started hanging at meetings with her mom. She heard her mother say in the *rooms* one day, "I go to church, to save my soul. I come to the rooms of recovery, to save my life." Gaváta got it !!! She understood. She then became a part of the EFFORTS family. Her favorite N/A meeting became the noonday fellowship at TRUST in Northeast, D.C. It was some fine brothers there with nice expensive rides. Gaváta was fresh out the penitentiary, single, celibate, God-fearing, 147 pounds and shoulder length hair. No one could tell her anything. If someone got her telephone number and attempted to make contact with her after 8 p.m. on their first call, she quickly dismissed them as no-good and only wanting one thing. Her standards was high. Prophetess Juanita Bynum had a video sermon called *No More Sheets* which was now embedded in her character and she realized her value and worth as a Woman of God. So with her mother on her arm in Sobriety and her new found relationship with Christ, the two of them were unstoppable. Grandma Madam had purchased Regina a couple of used cars. Their favorite was the convertible, so together they enjoyed their days by running errands for Granny, hanging at EFFORTS, in N/A Meetings, and eating.

CHAPTER 32

Over time, it was evident that even though Regina wasn't using the physical drug, many of her manipulative and get-over behaviors had not changed. Everyone understood that this would take time and that trust would have to be reestablished. Rob would often say things to anger Gaváta and try to throw monkey wrenches in their new found mother-daughter relationship, but they'd find a way to quickly deal with them and move on. He envied their 'holy rolling' to church and revivals all the time, and how Granny, Regina, and Gaváta would often talk about the pleasure of four generations, (Woo made the 4th Generation in the house), of McCollough women having quality time laughing and getting to really know who one another is all over again. He'd expose how Regina stole and sole valuable souvenir postage stamps and coins out of Sissy's cleaners when they cleaned out the Dry Cleaners after her death. He revealed that Regina's home phone was fraudulent and listed in Sissy's name. A $5,000 platinum ring that Sissy was holding for Gaváta which she had purchased for Big Carlos, even came to surface after no one claimed to have seen it. Sure, Gaváta felt betrayed and even had a tantrum, but her relationship with her mother, was more valuable, so Grandma Madam quickly intervened and they made amends. In the beginning, there were even times Granny would send Regina to the bank and she was still changing the amounts on checks instead of just asking. Old habits die hard, but eventually she stopped and realized that her behavior was unnecessary.

CHAPTER 33

In 2003 things were really good for Regina, Gaváta and most of the family in that they were heavily involved in the affairs of the church and simply just trying to do the right thing.

That August, Gaváta's beau, Robert "Tubby" King, a man unconnected to the church in any way, was called out by Bishop S.C. "Sweet Daddy" Madison, during the Convocation season in Baltimore, Maryland, to be a preacher in the Apostolic United Church.

September 2003, they were married in Fairfax, Virginia, and with her second marriage, she had then become a preacher's wife. They traveled with Grandma Madam, her entourage, Regina, and Jiamé all throughout the east coast enjoying worshipping in various services together.

The following year during the business week of Convocation in Washington, D.C. both Gaváta and Regina were ordained Local Missionaries of The Apostolic United Church. They received their authorization letters only after being asked to recite The Apostolic United Church Creed in front of the Council. In their nervousness, they stumbled through it, but did it together. What was ironic was that Regina was the director of the Youth Choir at Marshall Heights and had made all of her grandchildren and everyone on the choir memorize it, but when it came time for her to say it aloud, her own thoughts went blank. So now they were both Missionaries, mother and daughter, put in office together, but not before Grandma Madam made the decision that it was high-time to get her girls together, in style. She co-signed for Gaváta a Mercury Cougar and Regina a Toyota Camry, both purchased directly off of the lots of their perspective brand-dealers. She even leased herself the newest Lincoln Town Car. Her nosey, controlling housekeeper tried to hinder and discourage her from doing such things, but Clara McCollough did what she wanted to do when she wanted to do it. They were gainfully employed and very capable of paying their own car notes. Furthermore neither of them wouldn't dare disappoint the trust that Granny had put in either one of them.

One night, Gaváta and Tubby was coming from Marshall Heights driving down Benning Road, Northeast. This is a long stretch. They noticed Regina's green Camry so they elected to catch up to it. When Tubby arrived along the side of Regina's car, they were at a red light and Gaváta's position in the passenger seat caused her to be the nearest to the Camry driver's side window. Jiamé was driving. Both Tubby and Jiamé, rolled down the electronic windows and Regina was leaned all the way back in the passenger's seat. When Vá attempted to speak and called for her mother to sit up so she could see her, Regina sat up to say hello and her whole face was surprisingly sunk in. As the light changed to green, and she processed what she had just saw, she roared in laughter. Tubby called Jiamé on the cell phone to try to make sense of what was just seen. When he hung up the phone, he looked at his wife and said, "Your mother is so hurt. She's crying because you laughed at her like that." Gaváta felt bad but in her silliness, she admitted to Tubby, "I just saw her yesterday and she didn't look like that. People should warn people before they go do crazy stuff to themselves." In her guilt, she asked her husband to go to Mom and Pop's house instead of straight home. When they arrived, Regina was still in the car and Gaváta approached her with an instantaneous sincere apology. "Ma, I am so sorry. Oh My God, What happened?" In spite of excruciating pain, stitches and through cotton balls, Regina went on to explain to her daughter that she had been using drugs for so long that the doctors said that the chemicals from the cocaine was so embedded in the bone of her teeth that she would never be able to have a clean urinalysis. Her mother wanted that out of her system for good and was *just* that serious about her sobriety, so she had all of her teeth taken out and they would be replaced with dentures. That was yet another remarkable moment when Gaváta realized how serious Regina really was about living a clean and sober life.

CHAPTER 34

Jiamé was released from federal prison in the fall of 2001 and it was everyone's bet that either he and Regina would divorce because he elected to continue to use drugs, or that she would relapse. No one really knew what would happen so it was a waiting game. He came home to their small one bedroom apartment that was in eye's view of Granny 24/7 which was located in the 200 block of Allison Street. Surprisingly, he followed suit and stayed clean. He quickly found employment and became the man of the house that he had never fully been. He embraced Christianity wholeheartedly and was an awesome husband to his wife. But Gaváta once again, had lost her mother. Regina tried hard to spread herself *thin* to keep everyone happy, but it was just a little too much. Gaváta began dating someone from the church who quickly asked her to be his wife. With the void she felt once again, she accepted his proposal but the marriage never came into fruition. After a few brass words and expressions of hurt feelings of abandonment, Gaváta moved out from Granny's house. First with her new fiancée. After leaving him she moved in with her sister Ruth and then finally into her own place. In her sassiness, she demanded all of her children to be in her home in spite of her recent release from prison. When she attempted to take RéJene, all hell broke loose. Grandma Madam, demanded Gaváta to come to her home immediately for an urgent meeting. With tears running down her face, she was summonsed by the Family Matriarch. Grandma Madam begged Gaváta not to take RéJene from Regina because the family felt that "RéJene was Regina's Recovery Baby, and the only reason that she had stayed clean." Gaváta would never intentionally hurt or defile her grandmother so her wish was granted and Woo *(RéJene)* remained in the care of her Grandma. Therefore, Regina and Jiamé had a child to raise together as their own.

CHAPTER 35

Grandma Madam's trust for Regina had really grown extensively within the first few years of her recovery. She added Regina to her accounts at Industrial Bank. This allowed her to be able to make both deposits and withdrawals for her mother. Regina received her own set of keys to Granny's home and was able to come and go as she pleased. She was both a fulltime wife and daughter. It was a beautiful sight to behold.

As Jiamé and Regina got settled into their place and the apartment became a home, they would sometimes have as many as ten of her grandchildren to stay over at once. They had regular Sunday family dinners. Everyone came. Sometimes it would be over thirty family members in their small cozy abode eating, talking, reminiscing and catching-up with the current events of their own personal lives. Both the children and the adults would have fun playing church, reliving unforgettable moments, times and services. Dancing, shouting, singing, playing the tambourine, someone emulating highlights of a sermon and a hilarious moment, imaginary shout-bands with imaginary trombones and chair seats with someone beating on as drums, tithes and offering collection, testimony service, a child fake-catching the holy ghost or speaking in tongues, -- these were all the joys that was shared in this small but loving space. Regina's *redeemed* status, was being embraced by the family without much effort on every level, -- from their emotions to their mental and psychological healing. She wanted to expeditiously get her family in order so that she could function as a real grandmother and an upcoming family matriarch. After dinner on Sundays, she would often take the 'hot-seat' in the middle of her living room floor, for everyone to express their hurts, issues or whatever they felt. She told them that this exercise was regularly practiced at the inpatient drug programs. All in attendance complied and it was quite healthy. After a few months, issues with other parties in the family surfaced and it was hard for them to assume the position in the 'hot-seat' especially not being forewarned about who would be pulled up and what about. It was a challenging thing to do, but everyone eventually got a turn and it actually wasn't as bad as it seemed. Regina's apartment became a mini N/A Meeting / Recovery House, more often than not. But, it was okay because the family felt excited about being able to experience her recovery process with her. At least most of them did...

Gaváta loved this new mother, but her siblings, Ruth and Rob would disrespect their mother and Jiamé and throw their past in their faces. Ruth would even allow her children to be disrespectful to their grandparents. The brother and sister duo, often spoke as if Regina owed them something. News Flash !!! They both were over age twenty-one with children. So for the baby of the family, Gaváta, to feel this way when she didn't rely solely on her mother after a 27 month prison bit, Gaváta's concerns were valid. With felonies on her record, Gaváta sought out further education, stayed employed, worked hard, saved, and pressed forward that much harder to be independent, even with pressing restitution obligations. Her lazy brother and sister needed to get over the past and forgive. They pretended to have it together. They claimed to have lived drug-free lives and to have been model parents to their children. So why did they lack in giving consistent encouragement and moral support to their mother instead of always being takers and looking for a reason to beg? Gaváta often told her mother that all that she owed her was to stay clean. She believed that if her mom stayed clean, she could assist her in every area of her life, primarily with love, spirituality and wisdom.

SECTION XVI:

THE FINAL TRIAL

CHAPTER 36

Gaváta felt that the ultimate test for Regina would be the loss of her mother. When Madam Clara McCollough died January 2012, she kept it together. She did not relapse or waver. In the months to follow, both close and extended family, and even members of the church, made her feel that she was unworthy of having a part of, or a say-so in the her mother's estate, after-death and probate affairs. As strong as she had been in staying clean, the harsh words of her past, pierced her deep and they hurt her badly. Gaváta was being housed in Patuxtent Maryland Prison Facility at the time, and when she called home and learned of the way her mother was being treated, it ached her heart ten times worse than the pain she felt when being told of her Granny's death. Her mother's words and cries on the other end of the phone, were aching heart vibrations. No hugs were even remotely possible at this moment. Words could not even suffice what Regina was trying to say that she was feeling. A compilation of guilt, grief, anger, regret, vengeance, and determination, was what Gaváta heard from her mother's heart. They were the words that couldn't be verbally conveyed. Of course, every devious and vengeful form of planning began to develop into Gaváta's mind of how to solve this uprising against her maternal best friend. With no chaplain even assigned to the facility to help Gaváta deal with her own grief, somehow, all of the religion, all of the praying, all of the reading of the Bible, all of the relationship she had been strengthening in with her Lord and Savior Jesus Christ, something overtook her *will*. She submitted to the guidance of the Holy Spirit and for the rest of that phone call, Gaváta encouraged and built her mother up. She empowered her with every solid word she knew. She assured her mother of how her past didn't matter, and that it only exuded the strength, endurance, and perseverance that she was capable of. By the end of the call, Regina had digressed and sounded peaceful. When Gaváta hung up, she continued to pray because she knew that things would only get harder before they got better. Moreover, she didn't want her mother to give up and have to get a new clean-date. And, she didn't. Regina endured. She did what was necessary for continued peace in her life and did not use again even after the loss of her mother and the pressures that followed. This once again made Gaváta proud.

SECTION XVII:

TODAY SHE IS ...

CHAPTER 37

———— ⁑ ————

Approaching the new year of 2015, [at the conclusion of writing this book] both Gaváta and Regina was able to look back and see the struggles, but appreciate the healing. Now there is sincere love, unity, and forgiveness that words cannot express.

Regina is now a Woman of God, who remains a Missionary of The First United Apostolic Church for All People. She is a drug addiction counselor and a sponsor to many. She sporadically facilitates N/A Meetings. She is a sought after speaker of *The Recovery Process*. She has dabbed in counseling for abused women with children. With twenty-seven grandchildren and a rapidly growing number of great-grands, she fulfills her daily obligation and commitment as a wife, mother, and friend. Regina successfully kept RéJene on the Honor Roll throughout most of her schooling and propelled her into the college life with every iota of support she could muster. Gaváta hurt-fully and regretfully admits that she herself failed at mothering Woo. But, somehow in that agony, she feel that her cataclysmic behaviors, opened the door to a small part of her mother's redemption, growth, and opportunity. When Regina got clean, Gaváta would often quote to her a scripture out of the Book of Joel in the Bible. The text of Joel 2:25 speaks of 'God restoring back the years that the enemy, *the cankerworm and the palmerworm and the locusts*, stole' from her. Gaváta would say something like, "Ma, so you used for twenty-four years, right? And you're about fifty-five now. And, since God's promises are true, you gotta live until you're at least 79 years old, right? Cuz, God gotta give you everything back." Regina would laugh and tell Gaváta how crazy she was, but she believed this promise, as it pertained to her mother. In raising Gaváta's baby girl, just as Gaváta was the baby girl; and then RéJene is the only one of Gaváta's four children that have dimples just like Gaváta, and who looks almost identical to Gaváta, not to mention that she was named in Regina's honor, -- How could it be viewed as anything more than Regina being granted a second opportunity to raise her baby girl?

One Saturday while they were out for breakfast, Gaváta remembered her mother sharing with her the blessing of having RéJene in her home. She told Gaváta that there were many days she thought of using again, but in order to get to the stairs, she had to pass by Woo's room. Looking at that little girl laying in the bed, knowing how much she loved and depended on her, would always cause her to retreat and to go back into her room and to somehow lose the thought of relapse. Expressing this reminded Gaváta of Jesus' commandment of love and how scripture says that "Love covers a multitude of sins". Regina's love for RéJene was yet another strengthening vessel to her sobriety walk.

Whenever speaking of her mother, Gaváta will profess to anyone without reservation that *her mother's testimony and sobriety* is the heart felt diamond that she wears wherever she goes...an unmovable, irreplaceable jewel.

Today, in Gaváta's eyes, her mother is and always will be the most perfect cut, pressure sustained, valuable, rare diamond that the world would ever be able to visually behold.

EPILOGUE

By Regina McCollough-Hargrove
Gaváta's Mother

I can usually concentrate when everyone who is about me is some-where in the house, other than in my space at that present time, and I think I do even better when it is "crunch time". It took the twirling "red and blue" lights on the 11th of December, 1999 for me to under-stand it was not yet time for "santa claus", and these were not the beautiful lights that topped the gold dome at the church. Neither were they the glorious colors of the stained glass windows of the sanc-tuary. I am sure that a Power Greater than sent this rescue vehicle known as a "squad car" to lock me up or down, but to save and answer some Christian prayers that had not given up on me. My children and grandchildren included.

For several city blocks, my entire life such as it was seemed to flash before me. The Bishop's only girl, Jiame's wife, my kids mom, grandma, ... And on and on and on, and then it hit me, 'it was time for me to sur-render, totally surrender'. I no longer wanted to be called six numbers, or by a cell block unit. But I was and could be better that what I now faced for the year of 2000. I was ready to go in my closet with a sincere heart, mind and soul. I was ready to ask God to take complete control. My mom needed her daughter, my brothers needed their sister, for sure, my husband needed his wife and "I" needed my offsprings, perhaps more than they needed me. But "I" for sure was ready. My journey on the road to becoming both clean and sober would only work if I was doing this for Regina 1st. My travel on this trickery starship, earth, was all in my God's hands now. I am completely willing to tell him when the windows of my life are cloudy, foggy, and sometimes broken. He continues to stay on the scalpel and he shows me daily that he is able and qualified to keep my life afloat. Thank you God for you angels, "grace and mercy" and for rescuing me. I feel that interstellar connection and touch of love and pride, because of prayer.

P.S. If you choose to live in my past, that's on you…. I don't live there anymore *(Author of quote Anonymous)*

ACKNOWLEDGEMENTS

To my dear grandparents, the late **Bishop Walter "Sweet Daddy" McCollough and First Lady St. Madam Clara B. McCollough**, I thank you for loving me an instilling the value of family, marriage, respect, love, education, ethics and teaching me who God really is.

To my beautiful mother, **Regina McCollough-Hargrove**, you are the reason for this book and your life is a big part of the passion of who I am becoming in ministry.

To my stepfather, **Jiamé J. Hargrove**, thank you for loving, being a daddy to my children and I, supporting me in every positive endeavor I embark upon.

To my four amazing children, **Isaiah, Christian, Carlos Jr., and RéJene** I am so proud of you all. You have so much talent and energy. Give it back to God and watch what he will do.

To my seven beautiful grandchildren, **Naomi, Zaye'Mari, Micah, Kamari, Armani, Chloe, and Serenity** welcome to a family of overcomers, love, anointing and victory.

To the late, **Mary "Aunt Sissy" Hill,** Thank you for loving, mothering, pampering and caring for me. You did it *all* from educating to nurturing me. I could only pray to be the woman you were with half the strength you had. I will always love you.

To my outstanding brothers **Anthony "Tony" Hart,** and **Bobby Smith Jr.,** in spite of what it looks like, anyone on earth would be blessed to have you both as brothers and best friends. Tony you always were there for me growing up and Bobby I couldn't be where I am today without you. You have been so instrumental in my life in the last 12 months. You both are a loving vessels. I am excited about what God is still going to do in your lives. Walk in your anointing and who God says that you are and never give up.

In remembrance of the late **Mary "Aunt Molly" Upshur** and **Thomas "Mike" Holman,** your Little Vá-Vá kept her head in the books just as you taught me to. Thank you.

To a loving - loyal Man who has watched me excel. Your presence and wisdom and gift of ENCOURAGEMENT are not to be taken for granted. You are a man that I will always honor and care for. **W. Tavon Johnson,** thank you for advising me, encouraging me and being a listening ear. You are truly a friend who has exuded a level of care *in* *action and deeds* while teaching me a lot, especially how to "slow down and calm down" and for sticking by me through the thick and thin.

To my dear friend, **Aaron Easterling,** you are a true friend, a confidant, a gift from God, and the most amazing fashion designer I know. The prophetic words that you have spoken over my life, have always come into fruition. Thank you for loving me and being there in my seasons of brokenness and excellence.

My irreplaceable Friend-Mentor, **Sirena C. Whittington,** thanks for never giving up on me and always praying for me and believing in me.

To the most vocally blessed roommate I could have ever hoped for, **Sha'mere Germany**, you pushed and force and encouraged me to write many nights when I felt way too tired. Thank you for pulling this out of me. Continue to sing for the Lord.

To the MCIW Warden, **Margaret Chippendale,** and the Administration. Thank you for trusting and believing in me and affording me the opportunity to give birth to this book, which will pour life and ministry in to many. I thank God for showing you who I have grown to be and who I continue to develop into, through him.

To the Derelicts of "35", **Charlene, B.J., Debbie, Renee, the late Loraine and Daddy Joe,** thank you for taking this sobriety walk with my mom so she'd have friends who understood her struggles in times when I could not.

To a man who has made a major impact in my life. You have enriched me with love, refueled me about visions and my purpose in life, and made me more passionate about restoration, forgiveness and the fact that life is way too short. **Mr. Michael Eugene Boone**, you will always be a special love and friend. You are far more than "my son's father", you absolutely exude the strength of life. Thank you for teaching me what true love and protection from a man should look like, very early in life.

To **Ms. Rudera Bailey,** a woman who nurtured me through my grandmother's death, Thanks for your consistent encouragement, in all but forcing me to write this book expediently, with hopes that it will restore the relationships with your adult children. If no one else grasps the purpose of this writing, I pray that your children will. God can heal and restore.

To the church in which I was raised and for whom my grandparents lived and died for, **The United House of Prayer for All People.** Thank you for instilling the Gospel through the Apostolic Faith in me. It's because of this foundation, that I have left religion and now have a relationship with Christ. It is He who has empowered me to walk in the purpose and anointing to which God called me.

To those who have poured into me spiritually giving me the necessary rebuke when needed. I can never thank you enough or tell you how much I appreciate you all. **Apostle Charles Leon "Uncle Buddy" McCollough, Maudrie "Aunt Maude" McCollough, Apostle R.C.**

Lattisaw, Rev. Cheryl Mercer, Rev. Lettie M. Carr, and Pastor Carole Cloud.

In addition to pouring into me and giving me the necessary rebuke, the four of you, additionally saw potential and gifts in me to enhance the body of Christ. In spite of my fears, you pushed me... **Rev. Chaplain Lettie M. Carr,** *my gifts of teaching, facilitating, and the birthing of the gift of MIME;* the late **Gwendolyn Shelton** (of Empowerment Temple, AME Church, in Baltimore, Maryland), **and** the late **Minister Ridia Reid,** *teaching;* and **Reverend Cheryl Mercer,** (of Greater Mt. Calvary Church, in Washington, DC), *a book to be written and walking in all that God has called me to be.*

To every ministry who has helped me to grow by television, radio broadcasts, books, or prison ministry, I thank you and couldn't have done this without your words of encouragement and instruction somewhere along the way. **Bishop T.D. Jakes, Pastor John K. Jenkins, Co-Pastor Evangelist Susie Owens, Prophetess Juanita Bynum, Joyce Meyer, Pastor Antione Hutchins, Bishop Noel Jones, Pastor Jamal Harrison Bryant, and Pastor Creflo Dollar.**

To my Present and Future parents in the Gospel, **Archbishop Alfred A. Owens and Co-Pastor Susie Owens,** if it had not been for the God in you; if it had not been for your remembrance of Matthew 25:35-45 and having the ability to effectively execute it in my brokenness, I know that FAILURE would have defeated me. But, because you feed me physically, spiritually and emotionally, then prayed for me and didn't give up on me, I am able to continue to grow and become all that God Ordained me to be. **I LOVE YOU BOTH !!!!**

DEAR READER:

If something in this book inspired you, I would love to hear from you. If you have read this publication and would like me to come and speak, mime or do a live book signing, you may contact me by:

Email: mym4Christ@gmail.com
Facebook: https://www.facebook.com/gavata.smith
LinkedIn: https://www.linkedin.com/in/
            gavata-smith-91b68b155/
Twitter: https://twitter.com/Gavata1
Website: https://gavata.org

ABOUT THE AUTHOR

———◆———

Gaváta is a native and current resident of Washington, D.C. She is the proud mother of four adult children and seven grandchildren. She is a member of Greater Mount Calvary Holiness Church and there she *Mime*s and attends Calvary Bible Institute. She is passionate about encouraging others, Public Speaking and is a Christian Educator {Approved through her 4 year education at Evangelical Training Association (ETA)}. Gavata has her Leadership in Ministry Degree from ETA. She has often been categorized as a "career student" and a "future preacher". Her spiritual gifting is that of Administration, Teaching, Apostleship, and Evangelism. In accepting that this all may be true, she stays faithful and loyal to all that God has both instilled in and revealed to her and the church home of GMCHC where God has strategically placed her. She continues to pray, worship, study and be of service.

Mym4Christ@gmail.com

CPSIA information can be obtained
at www.ICGtesting.com
Printed in the USA
LVHW051544131118
596831LV00002B/246/P

9 781545 649060